The Power of Identification with Christ

Mark Hankins

The Power of Identification with Christ

Mark Hankins

The Power of Identification With Christ

1st printing, Copyright © 1996 by Mark Hankins

Published by MHM Publications

Mark Hankins Ministries

PO Box 12863

Alexandria, LA 71315

www.markhankins.org

Table of Contents

The Plan of Identification

The Power of Identification

The Pursuit of Identification

INTRODUCTION
CALLING THE COYOTES

Several years ago in Arizona, I went coyote hunting with an avid hunter. We got up very early in the morning while it was still dark and put on all of our camouflage — pants, shirt, hat, and boots. My shotgun and pistol were also camouflaged. Even my hands and face were covered with camouflage paint. My friend also gave me a pair of camouflage glasses with a camouflage veil. I was so camouflaged, when I looked in the mirror, I couldn't even see myself!

We sat on a mountainside on the ground under a big bush with camouflage netting wrapped around us. My friend then began to call the coyotes. He had a little wooden call that he put to his mouth and blew. The call made a loud squealing noise like the sound of a wounded rabbit. The idea was that when the coyotes heard the squeal of the hurt rabbit, they would come for what they thought was a nice meal.

My friend and I stayed under the bush for several hours calling the coyotes. I started to feel pretty ridiculous because we were two grown men dressed like "Rambo" sitting under a bush making crazy noises.

WOUNDED RABBIT CALL

We did not get a coyote that day, but I learned a valuable lesson. The Lord began to talk to me about faith. Many people, even Spirit-filled Christians, are continually whining and speaking words of defeat and depression, calling up the coyotes of failure. Their "wounded rabbit call" attracts the devil. He comes to devour them. It is open season on the person who whines, complains, and constantly speaks of fear and failure.

That kind of attitude opens the door to the devil. We have many "wounded rabbits" in the church who need to change their sound. I don't believe the devil can kill anyone anytime he wants. He has to get us to agree with his doubt and fear before he can do us any harm.

Faith agrees with God and shuts the door on the devil. By changing your sound to a bold declaration of who you are in Christ Jesus, you will begin to attract the blessings of God in a greater measure.

ACKNOWLEDGING YOUR
IDENTIFICATION IN CHRIST

How does someone change a life-long habit of wounded rabbit language? One good place to begin is Philemon 6, "That the communication of thy faith may become effectual by the acknowledging of every good thing which is in you in Christ Jesus." We need to acknowledge our identification with Christ by boldly saying, "The Lord is my helper, and I will not fear...," (Hebrews 13:6). I am who God says I am. I have what God says I have. I can do what God says I can do.

Many good things are in us that are in Christ. The Apostle Paul says that our faith will become effective by acknowledging every good thing that is in us in Christ. We will no longer have the cry of defeat, fear, and doubt. By acknowledging our identification with Christ, we will begin to make the sound of victory, prosperity, and blessing.

The Plan of
Identification

1

IDENTIFICATION, IDENTIFIED, IDENTICAL, IDENTITY

Have you ever checked in for a flight and been asked for proof of identification? You can say, "Here I am. Can't you see — this is me. I can prove that I exist. Just look." The authorities want to see a passport or driver's license. You cannot prove who you are without presenting official identification.

Even when I played baseball in elementary school, they wanted to see my birth certificate! I could have said, "Look, I can prove I was born. Here I am." That was not enough; I needed some authentic, legal, official proof that I was who I said I was. To transact business at a bank, we must also have some identification. This is all a part of life in this natural world.

In the realm of the Spirit you say, "Well, here I am. Obviously, I am who I am." God will ask, "Do you have any identification on you?" You say, "I sure do, I have some identification right here in Galatians 2:20, 'I am crucified with Christ: nevertheless I live; yet not I, but Christ liveth in me....' That is my identification with Christ. I am with Him. I have some identification on me."

Spiritually speaking, all of us must carry some identification to do business in the realm of the Spirit. The Word of God must be engrafted into our inner man so we know who we are in Christ. We must also carry the Bible as our official, legal identification. We must also carry the anointing of the Holy Spirit as the guarantee that we are who God says we are and we have what God says we have. Even the devil knows who you are when you have been born again and washed in the blood of Jesus.

Acts 19:13-16 tells the story of the seven sons of Sceva who tried to cast out devils in the name of Jesus "whom Paul preacheth." The demons said, "Jesus we know and Paul we know, but who are you?" Jesus had official identification in Heaven and hell — so did Paul. You and I can also know who we are and the authority that is ours in Christ. It is more than just trying to be religious or using religious words. It is your identity. It is official, legal, and authentically recorded in your own heart as well as in Heaven and hell. We carry the Word of God and the anointing of the Holy Spirit as official identification.

IDENTIFYING YOURSELF

The words: identification, identity, identical, identified are all related to each other. *Identification* is defined in Webster's Dictionary as: considering or treating as the same; the condition or fact of being the same in all qualities under consideration. Many people live and die and never really find their true identity. Often people never figure out who they are, so they act like someone else. They act like the strongest personality around. Some identify with someone on television who made an impression on them. They try to talk, dress, walk, or do their hair like that celebrity. Others pick a sports figure, singer, cowboy, or gangster. Some identify with a problem that they have had and call themselves by that name, such as divorced, alcoholic, or bankrupt. However, there is a stronger identification than what has happened to us naturally.

Some people's only identity is wrapped up in their profession. They live for their work. They identify more with what they do than what they are. They say, "I am a mechanic," or "I am a secretary." Your identity must be greater than just what you do. Your identity is who you are.

Some people identify with their jobs so strongly that if they were to lose their job, they would lose their identity. If they lose their job as a fireman, after being a fireman all their life, they may have an identity crisis. They have said, "I am a fireman" for years. No, "fireman" might be what you do, but you are not a "fireman."

Let's go a step further. Some people just identify with their race and cannot get past the color of their skin or their racial or national ancestry. They say, "I am Hispanic," "I am white," "I am Asian," or "I am black." Then they describe themselves and their strengths or weaknesses by their physical appearance or racial identity.

My parents did not let me think that way. I was not allowed to judge people according to their skin. Actually, I am not really all white, I am polka-dotted because I have freckles!

Some people want to study their ancestral roots to find out who they are. If they go far enough, they will go back to Adam. People who study their family trees need to be careful because all they may find is a bunch of nuts!

In my family line, we have some Indian, some German, some Scottish, and who knows what else. Most people are not truly one race or nationality. They just identify with a certain race. Your body does have some forms of identification, but your spiritual identification is stronger than your physical identification. In Christ, there is a whole new race. In Him, you are a brand-new creation.

There is some validity to your natural identification, but there is an even greater validity in your spiritual identification. Maybe what has happened naturally to you has had a great impact on your life, but what happened to you through Jesus is greater than anything else that has ever happened to you. When you see what God has done for you in Christ, the reality of redemption will swallow up your old identity.

START DRILLING

I once read a story about a strange happening in south Louisiana by Charles Perrow in his book, "Normal Accidents."

Texaco was drilling for oil in Lake Peigneur in southern Louisiana. The drill was down 1,250 feet when it got stuck...One hour later the men noticed that the rig was listing badly, and they abandoned it. Watching from the shore they were surprised to see it sink from sight... Meanwhile, men working in a salt mine, part of which extended under the lake about 1,300 feet below it, noticed that their area of the mine was flooding, and they sounded the alarms. All fifty-one of them managed to escape as water rushed into caverns that were 80-feet high and as wide as a four-lane highway. Meanwhile, on the surface, a whirlpool threatened some early morning fishermen, and eventually pulled in some barges and a tug associated with the drilling. The whirlpool grew in size until it pulled in 65 acres of the Rip Van Winkle Live Oaks Gardens, a tourist attraction...After seven hours, the entire lake, once about one mile by two miles, had drained into the salt mine.

Here an oil rig, a salt mine, an entire lake, and 65 acres of land disappeared. When you drill into the phrase "in Christ" found in the New Testament, it swallows up your past, your failures, and your old identity. What God did in Christ is big enough to swallow up what you used to be. The unseen will swallow up the seen. The grace of God is bigger! In every case, what happened to you in Christ is bigger than anything else that has ever happened to you. What happened in the death, burial, and resurrection of Christ will swallow up anything that has happened to you.

What do you need to do? Get the drill out and start drilling. Drill in Galatians 2:20 and in Romans 6:6. Then drill in Ephesians 2:4,5 and in Galatians 6:14. Drill until you hit something in the realm of the Spirit that is bigger than anything that has happened naturally in your life. You will hit something in the realm of the Spirit that will swallow up your past. It will swallow up any disaster. Not only what happened to you in the past will disappear, but the smell of it will also be gone.

T.D. Jakes said, "You may have done what they said you did, but you are not who they say you are." Just because something has happened to you does not mean that is who you are. Your identity is different than your behavior.

We can never rise in life above our own understanding of who we are. Therefore, it becomes vital for us to understand who God says we are and what God says we have. The revelation of our identity in Christ Jesus is stronger than any other identification we have embraced in our lives. God identified us with Christ in His incarnation, His death, burial, resurrection, and His seating in Heaven. Therefore, the strongest revelation in the Bible is who we are in Christ Jesus!

Really, your true identity is who God created you to be. You will never find your identity until you find out who you are in Christ. Once you find out who you are in Christ, you will find your real identity.

CHANGE YOUR NAME, CHANGE YOUR IDENTITY

Many people have an identity crisis because there are so many voices trying to tell them who and what they are from the time they are born. However, since God is our Creator, He reserves the right to tell us who we are and what we are like.

Throughout the Bible, we can see God changing people's identities. Sometimes they did not even recognize who God said they were. Sometimes we have heard so many things and believed so many things about ourselves that when God tells us who we are, we are suprised.

God called Gideon "a mighty man of valor" when he was defeated and hiding from the enemy. Often God calls us something even though there is no physical evidence to support it, but He is God. He reserves the right as our Creator to reveal to us how He sees us and what He sees in us. He changed Abram to Abraham, "father of many," when he had no children.

He changed Abraham's identity and destiny. Sarai was changed to Sarah, "princess." Jacob, "deceiver," was changed to Israel, "prince of God." They had to have an identity change to carry the spiritual inheritance God wanted them to carry. We all must have an identity change to fulfill the destiny and dream God has for us.

We see Jesus in the New Testament changing people's identities. Simon was changed to Peter, "a piece of the rock," which is the revelation of who Jesus is. When Peter got the revelation of who Jesus was, he looked at Jesus and said, "Thou art the Christ...," Matthew 16:16-19. Really what Peter said was, "I finally found out who You are. You are not Elijah, You are not Isaiah, and You are not just a prophet. You are the Christ, the Messiah. You are the Anointed One who is spoken of in the Old Testament scriptures, the promised Messiah. Thou art the Christ, the Son of the Living God!"

Jesus turned around, looked at Peter, and said, "Flesh and blood did not reveal this to you. My Father revealed this to you. This is not common knowledge. You did not pick it up with your physical senses. You must have had some other kind of information. God must have shown it to you."

Right after Peter identified Jesus, Jesus identified him and said, "Thou art Peter, and upon this rock I will build my church; and the gates of hell shall not prevail against it" (v. 18). Jesus changed Peter's name, character, destiny, and possibilities. Everything changed once he identified Jesus.

So you can say to Jesus, "Thou art the Christ," and He will tell you exactly who you are. He will even change your name.

The moment we see who Jesus is, He tells us who we are. Saul of Tarsus' name was changed to the Apostle Paul. He went on to write more than half of the New Testament. These are a few of the radical changes God did in the lives of people. God is the original "people person." He actually holds the copyright for humanity! He is the original manufacturer and He can re-manufacture, remake, or reveal to you who He says you are. Do not let anyone else tell you who you are or what you are like. Only God has the right to determine your true identity.

2

FIRST ADAM, LAST ADAM

Your identification with Christ is really based on several spiritual laws. The whole Bible is really about two men — the first Adam and the last Adam. The "old man" is from Adam. Your first birth identified you with Adam. The entire human race is produced by Adam. The "new man" is Christ, who is called the "last Adam."

Everybody in the human race originated from the Garden of Eden and out of the first Adam. Your nationality, where you live, or what language you speak does not matter. Everyone came out of Adam and his wife, Eve. You could not have come into this earth any other way except through Adam's lineage, and you cannot get into Heaven any other way except through Christ.

One man, Adam, affected everyone who was ever born. Adam's sin affected the whole human race. The Apostle Paul said in Romans 5:17, "Through one man's dis obedience all were made sinners." When Adam disobeyed God, it affected everybody because everyone was in him when he sinned. We all came out of Adam. Often people think when they disobey God, they are only disobeying God for themselves. They say, "It is me. It is my life. I can do what I want to do." Really, what you do affects a lot more than just who you are. When you choose to disobey God, your disobedience affects your family, your children and your children's children.

However, when you choose to obey God, it also affects your family and those future generations in you. Through Adam — through one man's sin and disobedience — we are all affected. One man got us into this mess, and one man can get us out!

A COPY OF THE MASTER

Let me illustrate it this way. Our ministry used to make audio cassette tapes and you would have to use a duplicating machine. You had a master tape that you put in the duplicating machine, and it made three copies. You could get more machines, hook them together, get your master tape, and make hundreds of copies. If you were at a convention, they would have one master tape of the speaker and make a copy for everyone who wanted one.

If the speaker clears his throat in the first five minutes or loses his voice after fifteen minutes, guess what would be on the copy? Whatever was on the master tape would be on the copy. The copy was an accurate duplicate of the master tape. Somone once said, "I got a bad copy." No, there was a bad master. In the Garden of Eden, Adam was doing really well. God made him the master. God put in Adam everything the whole human race could want — joy, blessing, and dominion. He crowned him with glory and honor. Adam and Eve had all these things. He called them man and woman and the two together had dominion. When Adam sinned, the "master" developed trouble or became defective. It was marred by sin, sickness, death, depression, and confusion — every kind of defect you can imagine.

Then Adam and Eve began to reproduce and make "copies." Those copies went all over the world throughout the history of man. One man messed up the whole thing! You can trace it all back to identification with that one man, Adam.

You could say, "It is not fair that one man could have this effect on every man. I did not choose to be born this way." That is the way God made it. The same law that allowed one man, Adam, to affect every man is also the same law that allowed Jesus Christ, the last Adam, to take the condition the first man Adam had of sin, the curse, shame, and death. He absorbed all that into Himself and died with it. In His resurrection, God deposited everything in Christ that He wanted in man. God put in Christ what He wanted in you.

He allowed His only Son to become a man, born of a woman, conceived by the Holy Spirit. God was manifest in the flesh and walked around here with us. Jesus Christ walked the earth. He came for three reasons. First, He came to reveal the goodness of God. Second, He came to destroy the works of the devil. Third, He came to die.

When you receive Christ, you get off the Adam machine. You are now on Christ's machine. What does that mean? Christ is the "master" now, and when you get on His machine, the power of His death erases your old condition. The power of His resurrection identifies you with a whole new humanity — a whole new creation. You are not the same person anymore! You can no longer identify just with your natural family, you are now identified with Christ!

A LAW OF IDENTIFICATION

How could Jesus Christ, one man, die on the cross and His death be for every man? It is simply a law of identification. We were all identified with one man, Adam, and affected by him. This one man affected every person. God simply took the same law that allowed one man, Adam, to mess up everyone, and allowed one man, Jesus Christ, to die for everyone.

Before Christ, you were identified with Adam. You shared his condition, his lack of fellowship with God, his inheritance, and his future. Paul says, "Through one man's disobedience all were made sinners," Romans 5:17. One man affected every man. This law of identification with Christ is also found in this scripture:

*For the love of Christ constraineth us; because
we thus judge, that if one died for all, then all
were dead. - 2 Corinthians 5:14*

*...to this conclusion have we come — One died
for the sake of all; in Him then did all die.
- Arthur S. Way*

ADAM — THE ARCHETYPE
OF MANKIND

Let me illustrate it this way. Adam was more than just one man. Adam was an archetype, or the "master" out of which the whole human race came. God did not create the whole human race at once. He created one man and one woman and gave them the capacity of pro-creation. God let Adam father His family.

When God wanted to make the whole human race, He said, "I am going to make Adam and I am going to make Eve. I am going to make everybody come out of them because I like them." He then created them, gave them dominion and He crowned them with glory and honor. He blessed them and gave them a wonderful body, a wonderful intellect, and a wonderful spirit.

God made them just the way He wanted everyone to be — blessed, happy, victorious, and prosperous! He gave them dominion, but then sin came in. When Adam sinned, his condition passed on to his children and his children's children. His condition was passed on until it reached you and me.

THE MYSTERY OF YOUR ORIGIN SOLVED

The mystery of how you were born into the world as damaged goods is solved in the Bible. Do not be like the teenager who told his daddy, "I didn't choose to be born." His dad answered, "If you would have asked, we would have said no!"

When facing problems, crises, and confusion in your life, you can look back and say, "I did not choose to be born. Why was I born this way? Why was I born in this place? Why was I born to these people? Why was I born with this condition?" Everyone is born with a bad condition; some are worse than others.

We see "crack" babies born because of something that their mom or dad did. We see children born with deformities and illnesses. People say, "See what God did." No, God did not do that. God never created a child that way. That condition came because of a choice that was made thousands of years ago. That condition came in because of sin and the devil.

Man is born with a spiritual condition that separates him from God. This condition came into the world because of Adam, sin, and the devil.

If your parents moved to Louisiana from Texas before you were born, their choice would affect the state you were born in. So you are not a Texan; you are a Louisianian. Why? Yet unborn, you were in your parents when they moved, whether they knew it or not. When they moved, their decision affected you.

Parents often make decisions that affect the way their children are born and the way they are raised. They make decisions, and that condition is passed on.

You were not born in the condition Adam was created in. You were born in the condition he passed on. He was created in a state of righteousness and holiness, having fellowship with God and dominion in the earth. When Adam sinned, he was separated from fellowship with God and passed from life to death. You were also born in that condition, so you have trouble from the day you are born.

ADAM WAS NOT DECEIVED

We understand from the scriptures that Eve was deceived by the serpent. Eve's sin did not affect the whole human race; Adam's sin did. Adam was not deceived. Adam knew exactly what he was doing when he disobeyed God. Adam knew the moment he took of the fruit of that tree, spiritual death would set in. He knew he would lose his authority, and it would affect the whole human race.

You may wonder, "Why did he do it, then?" He looked at Eve, and she was beautiful. He looked at God. God said, "Thou shalt not eat of this tree." Adam actually decided to go with his wife instead of obeying God.

When God judged Adam and Eve, He judged them differently. Adam knew what he was doing and he carried the responsibility as head of the family. God had said, "You are supposed to take care of this garden. You are supposed to keep it and tend it." Adam's job was actually to guard the garden, to take dominion, and to keep the devil out of it. Adam reneged on his authority and allowed his wife to be in a place she should not have been, listening to the devil. Adam's negligence and disobedience caused man to lose dominion.

Many conditions have been passed on from Adam. These seeds that have been planted in the human race caused the destruction of man, his body, his dominion, and his authority. Your first birth into earth put you in Adam, and you are identified with Adam.

THE HOPE OF MANKIND

There is no hope for man's condition without Jesus Christ. There is no hope for man outside of the blood of Jesus and His death, burial, and resurrection. Man's condition cannot be corrected by reading a book or trying to do better. He cannot correct his behavior. He is a sinner by nature, and he cannot change himself. Only the blood of Jesus and the power of the Gospel can change a person. A person has to be born again if they are going to get out of Adam. They have to lose their identity in Adam and get identified with Christ, the last Adam.

In Christ, you establish a whole new identity that changes you, your thinking, your direction, and everything about you. You are not in Adam anymore; you are in Christ. You must be born again. You have to walk out of Adam and walk into Christ. The first Adam made a mess out of things, so God made a whole new Adam — Jesus, the last Adam. Jesus absorbed the condition of the first Adam. He took Adam's condition into Himself and died with it. He did this so that the moment you receive Jesus Christ by faith, His death becomes your death; His burial becomes your burial; His resurrection becomes your resurrection; His righteousness is your righteousness; His ascension is your ascension; His victory is your victory; His seating is your seating; His life is your life; His blessing is your blessing. Everything that God put in Him now comes into you.

This changes your identity. No longer can you identify with defeat because you are identified with the triumph of Christ. No longer can you identify with failure, sickness, and bondage because you are identified with Christ.

When a condition from your natural family comes, instead of saying, "That is me," you can now say, "I do not accept that condition. I cannot identify with it because I identify with Christ. I died with Christ. I was buried with Christ. I was raised with Christ. I identify with His triumph and His blessing. I am identified with Christ. That is who I am, and that is what I have. I do not accept that condition anymore."

It does not matter what your parents did, what neighborhood you came from, what runs in your family, or what people have been saying about you. Once you get in Christ, your whole identity is changed. You were identified with Adam before, but you are not in Adam now — you are in Christ!

3

OUR IDENTIFICATION
WITH CHRIST

I heard the story of a fireman in California whose hand was so severely burned, that his doctors determined they would have to amputate. One of the doctors, however, wanted to try an experimental surgery. He knew that the body has certain regenerative powers. He cut the man's side open and inserted the burned hand in his side for a period of time. To the doctor's amazement, when they removed the fireman's hand from his side, it had begun to heal and grow new skin.

I believe God did a similar surgery with man. When Adam sinned, man's condition looked so bad, it looked like God would have to amputate; but God had a plan of redemption. He performed supernatural surgery on the cross. He cut open Jesus' side and put us "in Christ." In Him, the power and the grace of God went to work and reversed the condition Satan caused. A new man was created — a man in Christ, a righteous man, a blessed man, a victorious man, a redeemed man, a healed man.

Now we are "grown together" — we are identified in Christ. Many scriptures use the terms "with Christ" or "with Him."

> *Knowing this, that our old man is crucified WITH HIM, that the body of sin might be destroyed, that henceforth we should not serve sin. - Romans 6:6*

> *But God, who is rich in mercy, for his great love wherewith he loved us, Even when we were dead in sins, hath quickened us together WITH CHRIST, (by grace ye are saved;) And hath raised us up together, and made us sit together in heavenly places in Christ Jesus. - Ephesians 2:4-6*

When Jesus was crucified, He took you with Him because He took your identical condition! As a matter of fact, when God saw Jesus on the cross, He saw your condition. Jesus literally took your sin, death, curse, shame, and condition. Since you were there in His death, you were there when God quickened Him and made Him alive. Both substitution and identification are involved. "Substitution" simply means He took your place and your condition. We progress from substitution to identification.

When God raised Christ from the dead, He quickened you with Him so you now have an identical life, identical righteousness, identical victory, identical blessing, and identical inheritance. As a matter of fact, you are one with Christ. You are joined to Him.

CRUCIFIED WITH CHRIST

Paul made some strange statements, didn't he? He said, "It is not me. Christ lives in me." In another place he said, "For me to live is Christ...," Philippians 1:21. He also said, "The mystery of the gospel and the glory of the gospel is Christ in you," Colossians 1:26, 27.

*I am crucified with Christ: nevertheless I live;
yet not I, but Christ liveth in me: and the life
which I now live in the flesh I live by the faith
of the Son of God, who loved me, and gave
Himself for me. - Galatians 2:20*

*I have been crucified with Christ. Now it is
not my old self, but Christ Himself who lives
in me. - Noli*

*I have been crucified with Christ. I live now not
with my own life but with the life of Christ who
lives in me. - Jerusalem Bible*

*Christ took me to the cross with Him, and I
died there with Him. - Laubach*

*I consider myself as having died and now
enjoying a second existence, which is simply
Jesus using my body. - Distilled Bible*

LITTLE I, BIG CHRIST

What does Paul mean, "I was crucified with Christ. It is no longer I that lives but Christ lives in me?" I like the way I heard T. L. Osborn say it a number of years ago, "Little 'I' moved out, and big Christ moved in." You could say it this way: "Weak 'I' moved out, and strong Christ moved in. Defeated 'I' moved out, and victorious Christ moved in. Sick 'I' moved out, and healed Christ moved in. Poor 'I' moved out, and rich Christ moved in. Cursed 'I' moved out, and blessed Christ moved in. I, in my little capacity and selfishness, moved out, and big Christ moved in." That is our identification with Christ.

You have been "twinned" with Christ. God did not do one thing in Christ and do something of a lower quality in you. God "cloned" you with Christ and made you identical to Him. He put the same righteousness, life, victory, blessing, and other qualities that are in Christ in your spirit.

How could you ever identify with defeat again when you are identified with Christ? You cannot identify with defeat because of the triumph of Christ. You have that in your genes. Your spirit has an instinct for life, victory, and triumph. You are a thoroughbred

— it is born in you. It is like a labrador retriever headed for water. He has to get in the water. It is in his genes. Likewise, victory is in your genes. You cannot explain it — it is just there.

When someone wants to buy a racehorse, they want to look at the mama and daddy. They want to trace that horse's lineage. They do not want a mule in there. You can take any old hound dog, but if you want a labrador, you want to know that dog is registered. You want to know if the seller has registration papers on him.

Your identification is not only in your genes, but God has papers on you. They have been recorded in the court house of eternity. They have been filed at the highest place in the universe. God said, "I have registration papers on you. You have been genetically re-created in Christ Jesus. You are a brand-new breed; a new creation in Christ. You have victory in you. You have righteousness in you. You have blessing in you. You cannot help it. When you get up in the morning, you just act like that. I bred you to win." Something in you says, "I am made to race. I am made to win!"

"FRANKENSTEIN" CHRISTIANITY

God has done this genetically. He is the original "people person." Science has never been able to create a human being. If you have watched horror movies, you have seen Frankenstein. Frankenstein is to man what religion would be to Christianity. Religion can produce something, but it is a monster with knobs on its neck!

Christianity is not man-made it is God-made. God has recreated or reproduced Himself and has made a new man. God has made a new creation. That new creation is a supernatural breed. It is not black, white, brown, Asian, or Hispanic. In that new supernatural breed is the last Adam, the head of the Church.

Throughout eternity, this new breed will just keep on going. God totally did away with the old race and the old Adam in you. He made a brand-new creation — a new creation with the triumph of Christ. Religion cannot do anything but leave you with knobs on your neck and stitches all around! If you look at people in all kinds of churches, you will see knobs all over their necks and stitches on their heads.

Christianity does not begin with something you do. Christianity begins with something God has done for you in Christ Jesus. God puts you in Christ. God identified you with Christ. God did it for you. Even before you were born, He saw you. He has a place for you to climb into in that rock, to get in His presence, and to see His glory. He will reveal Himself to you in Christ. God did that for you. God identified you with Him. Paul said, "I was crucified with Him." "With Him" reveals that Christ took you to the cross with Him.

DEATH AND RESURRECTION PROCESS

Theologians ask, "How could Paul say he was crucified with Christ when Paul was not even in Jerusalem when Jesus was crucified?" So how could Paul say he was crucified with Christ?

This has led some preachers and theologians to say that in Galatians 2:20, Paul is talking about a spiritual state he has somehow attained after thirty years of serving God. Be careful — we are getting into a Frankenstein religion here.

When you think this way, somehow you are trying to be identified with Christ, but you are right back in Jerusalem at the Church of the Holy Sepulcher where there is neither life nor glory. It is a big church with priests in long robes walking around in a circle day after day in a procession, swinging incense and saying, "We are trying to identify with the death, burial, and resurrection." That is why it is called the Church of the Holy Sepulcher. They believe the whole death and resurrection process happened in that spot, so pilgrims come and line up behind them in the procession.

When I went to Israel, they asked, "Does anybody want to get in the procession?" I did not get in the procession because it is a Frankenstein religion — a dead religion. It is man's attempt to be accepted by God, struggling to somehow identify with Christ.

In Israel, tourists go on tours to the Via Dolorosa, the Way of Sorrows. Tour guides tell you, "This is what happened to Jesus here, and this is what happened to Jesus there." They say, "Here is where He fell down, here is where He was crucified, and here is where He was buried." On the Via Dolorosa people try to identify with Christ.

People wear crosses around their necks to identify with Christ. They put pictures of the crucified Christ on their walls. They buy worthless things for a lot of money to identify with Christ. They want to own a piece of the rock at the nativity cave from Israel, the birthplace of Jesus. They buy water from the Jordan

River. They buy olive oil from Israel, but all they have is a Frankenstein religion with stitches and knobs on them. They are trying to identify with Christ.

REVELATION KNOWLEDGE

Paul was not talking about some spiritual state that he had struggled to attain after thirty years. What Paul was talking about was a different kind of knowledge. It is not sense knowledge. He said, "You did not see me there physically. I was not in Jerusalem physically, but by revelation knowledge, I know in God's eyes and in the mind of God, I was there. Through revelation knowledge, I know when Jesus died, I died. When He was buried, I was buried. When He was made alive, I was made alive. When He was raised, I was raised with Him. When He sat down, I sat down with Him. God saw me there. Everything Jesus did, He did it for me."

How can you be there? Because the death and resurrection of Christ were planned by God and prophesied thousands of years before they ever happened. Abraham enacted the whole drama on Mt. Moriah before it ever happened. He was willing to offer Isaac on an altar, but God said, "Jehovah-

Jireh is in these hills. The provision of God shall be seen," Genesis 22:13. There was a ram on that hill for Abraham's sacrifice, and that same hill is where Jesus was crucified thousands of years later.

Golgotha is the redemptive center of the world. What happened on the cross is an eternal God-event. God prophesied it, and God did it. We give it a time and a place for historical purposes, but in the realm of eternity, it is an eternal God-event that can be visited at any point and time as though it were happening right then.

When you get in the Spirit, instead of seeing your death, shame, guilt, sorrow, sickness, and poverty, you can see your condition in Christ and the fact that you were crucified with Him. When you get in the Spirit, you can say, "That was my death. I was there."

If you were there in His crucifixion, you were also there in His resurrection. How can you say you were there? By revelation knowledge. That is where God's genetic engineering takes place.

The same power that is in these events is also in the message. This was revealed when the centurion said, "...but speak the word only, and my servant shall be healed," Matthew 8:8. The Word carries the identity of Christ. You have been born again of an incorruptible seed that carries the identity of Christ in it. When that germ, seed, or sperm gets in your spirit you have been regenerated. You have been born of an incorruptible seed, a supernatural seed — the Word of God. You have been recreated.

How can Paul say that he was crucified with Christ? The old song says: Were you there when they crucified my Lord? Were you there when they laid Him in the tomb? Were you there when He rose up from the grave? Sometimes it causes me to tremble.

People say, "I could not have been there. I would have to be 2,000 years old to have been there." However, you and I were there. Paul was there. How could we have been there? Revelation knowledge reveals that we were there.

A PICTURE OF REDEMPTION

The New Testament gives us an explanation of how we are redeemed or God's method of redemption. Paul is the one who was chosen by God to explain redemption, and his letters are really the only ones that use the two words "in Christ" or "in Him."

The Apostle Paul said many things that people are still trying to figure out. What in the world is he talking about? How could you be in Christ? What does "in Christ" mean? Paul got this phrase from the Lord Jesus Christ. He did not think it up. Jesus came and visited Paul in Arabia and gave him the phrase "in Christ."

Paul said at the end of his ministry in Philippians 3:8,9: "...that I may...be found in him." If you want to find who you are, your true identity, and what you have, you will find it in Him. Paul said, "I am found in Him."

> *And be found in him, not having mine own righteousness, which is of the law, but that which is through the faith of Chris, the righteousness which is of God by faith.* —*Philippians 3:9*

IN THE ROCK

We have a picture of this in the Old Testament in Exodus 33:18-23. Moses says, "God told me to do these things and lead a million people, but I need some help. It gets rough out here. Show me your way." Then Moses adds, "Lord, I want You to show me your glory. Show me your glory."

God told Moses, "There is a place by me. When I pass by, I am going to put you in a cleft of the rock. When my glory passes by, you will not see anything except my back parts." Many times people get in the glory and think, "Whoo, I really have something here." All you have is just an after-effect. God went by ten minutes ago, and you are just getting the after-shock.

Moses wanted to see the glory of God, so God placed him in a hole, or a cave, or a cleft in that rock. Moses must have been inside that rock. He was filled with expectation because God was showing him His glory. Moses was inside of that rock, and he was saying, "Oh, oh, oh, this is going to be good!"

THE GLORY OF GOD

The Bible says that when God passed by, He said, "My glory is made up of all of my goodness. I am going to make all of my goodness pass before you, and I am going to The Power Of Identification With Christ 40 41 proclaim the name of the Lord. I am going to pronounce my name for you." In that place in the rock, in the glory of God, there are two main ingredients: the goodness of God and the revelation of who God is.

The goodness of God is exceeding abundantly above anything else. It is more than enough, and you say, "That is too much for me. God is too much. It makes me want to run and dance." Most people put limits on how good God can be to them. God wants to be so good to you that you are amazed all the time!

GOD IS ALL YOU NEED

When God said, "I will proclaim or I will pronounce my name," I do not know exactly what Moses heard, but in the name of God is the revelation of Himself, His character, and His person. Moses may have heard the names Elohim, the Creator; El Shaddai, the God who is more than enough; or Jehovah-Rapha, Jehovah-Shammah, Jehovah-Nissi, or some other name of God. When Moses heard all that, he said, "God, I will never need anything else but You. If I have You, I have everything!"

For Moses to see that glory, he had to get in that place in the rock. There is a positioning for the glory. You could say it is a place of grace where God Himself put Moses. Your identification with Christ or who you are in Christ begins with the grace of God. God puts you in a place where you can see His glory, get in His presence, know Him, experience Him, and enjoy Him.

In Exodus 33:18-23, there is a rock. That rock is Jesus! You are in the rock. Peter got the same revelation in Matthew 16:15-19, when he said, "You are the Christ, the Son of the living God." Jesus said, "And thou art Peter, and upon this rock I will build my church...." What Jesus said was that this rock is the revelation of who Christ is, and Peter is a piece of that rock.

When you get a revelation of who Christ is, you will recognize you are in union with Him. You are a piece of the rock, and you are identified with Christ. You share the same righteousness, the same life, and the same blessing. You are joined to Him — a piece of the rock in Him.

Psalm 32:7 says, "Thou art my hiding place; thou shalt preserve me from trouble; thou shalt compass me about with songs of deliverance." Climb into that place in Christ and the devil cannot harm you. Climb up into the grace of God, into the righteousness that is yours. Climb into place and say, "By faith I am climbing up into the place of who I am in Christ, and I am hearing some singing right now all around me songs of deliverance. Hallelujah! You are my hiding place."

4

FOUR LAWS OF
IDENTIFICATION

LAW ONE: THE LAW OF
REVELATION KNOWLEDGE

The Bible is more than just theology and history. The Bible is inspired by God and is God-breathed. God's Word is alive, and you can find yourself in the Bible.

Sense knowledge contacts the physical, but revelation knowledge shows you what God sees. When you see it in the Word, you can say, "I am who God says I am." You identify or find yourself in the Word. Revelation knowledge is how God changes people's identities.

Through revelation knowledge in the Bible, God can carry on two conversations at once. In other words, He could have been talking a thousand years ago and all of a sudden you read it, and the Holy Spirit says, "He wrote that for you." This is demonstrated in the Gospel of Luke when Jesus preached His first message in His hometown of Nazareth.

> *And there was delivered unto him the book of the prophet Esaias. And when he had opened the book, he found the place where it was written, The Spirit of the Lord is upon me because he hath anointed me to preach the gospel to the poor; he hath sent me to heal the brokenhearted, to preach deliverance to the captives, and recovering of sight to the blind, to set at liberty them that are bruised, To preach the acceptable year of the Lord, And he closed the book, and he gave it again to the minister, and sat down. And the eyes of all them that were in the synagogue were fastened on him. And he began to say unto them, This day is this scripture fulfilled in your ears. - Luke 4:17-20*

We know Jesus was God manifested in the flesh. We know He is deity, but Philippians 2:5-8 says He laid aside His powers of deity and functioned as a man. He was not born quoting scripture. He had to grow up as a child, a teenager, and a young man: "And Jesus increased in wisdom and stature, and in favour with God and man" Luke 2:52.

FIND YOURSELF IN THE BIBLE

Jesus studied the scriptures and found the places which referred to Him. For example, He found Isaiah 61:1-3 and recognized Himself in the Word of God. In His first sermon He said, "That is Me. Isaiah 61:1-3 is talking about me!" The Holy Spirit in Him and on Him increased dramatically as He identified with these scriptures. Although Isaiah had written that passage 700 years before, Jesus said, "That is Me...that is who I am...that is what I have...today this scripture is fulfilled!" We, too, must find ourselves in the Word of God. The Bible is God talking to us.

John the Baptist must have done something similar in Luke 3:4, "As it is written in the book of the words of Esaias the prophet, saying, The voice of one crying in the wilderness, Prepare ye the way of the Lord, make his paths straight." John must have studied the scriptures and found himself in them. When he read Isaiah 40:3, he must have said, "I am that voice! That is talking about me!" His true identity was in the Word of God. This is the Law of Revelation Knowledge.

As mentioned earlier, the Apostle Paul says something similar in Philippians 3:9, "And be found in him...." Paul, speaking of his relationship and fellowship with Jesus after thirty years of world-changing ministry, simply says, "I want to be found in Him." Paul found his true identity in Christ. If you have lost your identity or destiny, it can be found in Him.

In whom are hid all the treasures of wisdom and knowledge. - Colossians 2:3

For in him dwelleth all the fullness of the Godhead bodily. And ye are complete in him.... - Colossians 2:9,10

Because Jesus is called "the Word" in John 1:1, you can find Him throughout the Word. To find yourself in Him, you have to find yourself in the Word of God. Jesus will walk off the pages of the Word of God and into your life! When you see who He is, He will tell you who you are.

The Apostle Peter had an experience like this in Matthew 16:16-18. When Peter got the revelation of who Jesus is, he said, "Thou art the Christ, the Son of the living God." Jesus said, "Peter, you did not get that from man or from your five senses. Only God could have revealed it to you." (This is my personal interpretation.)

"And I say also unto thee...." Jesus is never finished when we get the revelation of who He is. He will always say something more to you. He has more revelation for you. There is more about who you are and what He has planned for you. Jesus said, "Thou art Peter...." Peter was changed by this experience. He must have thought about it every day after that. He had discovered his identity.

We see later that Peter's identity was challenged by his own failure when he denied Jesus. God's revelation for you will always be challenged, but the Word is still true. The Word will bring you through every challenge victoriously. We see Peter's identification clearly realized in the Book of Acts.

LAW TWO: THE LAW OF IDENTIFICATION

The whole Bible is about two men — the first Adam and the last Adam. The first Adam sinned and affected every man.

Your first birth puts you in Adam; your new birth puts you in Christ. Adam is the old man, and Christ is the new man. As we shared the same "identical" condition with Adam, we share the same "identical" condition with Christ. The Apostle Paul explains this in Romans 5 and 6.

What Satan did in Adam, God reversed in Christ. The first Adam got us in this mess, and every one of us is identified with Adam through the second law - The Law of Identification. You can find Adam's condition in any race or whatever language you speak — Spanish, Japanese, Korean, Swahili, English. Anywhere you go, you can still find Adam talking. He is saying, "I am sick. I am poor. I am confused. I am depressed. I want to kill myself. I want to kill somebody else." You can find Adam's language everywhere because the whole human race is identified with Adam. You can trace your family tree all the way back to Adam.

Jesus said, "You must be born again," John 3:7. God has two Adams: the first Adam and the last Adam. The first birth is in Adam. The second birth, when you are born again, puts you in the new Adam, and you are a new creation.

The Law of Identification is "Adam in Christ." One man got us in this mess, and one man can get us out. This is seen in Galatians 2:20.

> *I am crucified WITH Christ: nevertheless I live; yet not I, but Christ liveth in me: and the life which I now live in the flesh I live by the faith of the Son of God, who loved me, and gave himself for me.*

This Law of Identification can also be seen in the following verses:

> *[And I pray] that the participation in and sharing of your faith may produce and promote full recognition and appreciation and understanding and precise knowledge of every good [thing] that is ours in [our IDENTIFICATION with] Christ Jesus.... - Philemon 6, Amplified Bible*

...in our behalf God IDENTIFIED Him with everything in the whole realm of sin in order that by trusting Him, we might become (recipients of) God's kind of righteousness.
- 2 Corinthians 5:21, Blackwelder

Our former evil IDENTITIES have been executed, so to speak. Our old rebel selves were exterminated and that leaves us no further role to perform as offenders. We were linked with the Divine Representative in death.
- Romans 6:6, Richert

NAMES AND IDENTITIES CHANGED

God changed people's names and identities throughout the scriptures. Remember He told Abram, "You are Abraham, the father of many. Your wife is Sarah, a princess." They must have had a good time calling each other "Father of Many" and "Princess." They started calling themselves what God called them. We ought to start calling each other, "How are you doing, 'Blessed'?" "How are you doing, 'Redeemed'?" You have been made righteous. You are who God says you are.

God changed Jacob's name to Israel after their little wrestling match. God said to Gideon, "You are a mighty man of valor" and changed his name to Jerubbaal, which simply means, "Let Baal plead for himself." Gideon received such a change of character and identity that he challenged Baal. "I dare Baal to mess with me!" Gideon shook that place up.

"Saul," the Spirit of God said in 1 Samuel 10:6, "...the Spirit of the Lord will come upon thee, and thou shalt prophesy with them, and shalt be turned into another man." Peter was changed from Simon to Peter. Jesus told him, "You are this way now, but the revelation of who Christ is and getting filled with the Holy Spirit is going to move you from the imputed to the imparted."

When Saul of Tarsus met Jesus, he was hit so hard, it knocked the "S" off the front of his name and put a "P" there. "Paul," Jesus said, "Your name is not Saul anymore. Your name is now Paul."

IDENTITY CHANGED

Do you know that your experience with Jesus can be so real, it changes your identity? You will even forget who you used to be. You will say, "Hey, I am a whole new person." People will come around and say, "I know you. I remember you." And you can say, "No, you don't know me. That person you knew died."

That is what happened to Brother Kenneth E. Hagin when he was just a teenager. He was sitting with his friends on the running board of an old truck one day after he had been born again. He was only seventeen. They said, "We remember you. Remember, Kenneth, when we used to break in that store and steal that candy?"

Brother Hagin said, "No, I don't know what you're talking about. That guy died." They said, "You didn't die; you're sitting right here. That's you right here." They walked off shaking their heads.

"So," he said, "as a teenager, I was able to stand alone because I knew I had been changed. I was a new creation in Christ; I had a new identity."

LAW THREE: THE LAW OF SUBSTITUTION

For the love of Christ constraineth us; because we thus judge, that if one died for all, then were all dead. - 2 Corinthians 5:14

Other translations say, "...if one man died the death of every man then every man died in Him." Jesus said the same thing in John 12:32, "If I be lifted up, I will draw all men unto me." That means what happened on the cross was substitution. Jesus was not a martyr; He was a substitute — one man who died for every man.

Jesus took our place. He took our curse and died our death. He took our condition so we could have His condition. He was identified with us. We were there in His death and resurrection. Because He died for us, we died with Him. Because He was raised for us, we were raised with Him. Everything Jesus did, He did for us and it is credited to our account as if we did it. Substitution progresses to identification and union with Christ.

The Roman soldiers could not kill him. Jesus said, "Nobody can take my life from Me." When it came time to go to the cross, He said, "For this hour I was born." Jesus was a substitute for mankind.

Everything else He did in His earthly ministry pointed to this hour. In the four Gospels, a disproportionate amount of space is given to the actual events of the death and resurrection of Christ. We have the Holy Spirit because of what Jesus did. He said, "I am going to ascend and sit down, and I am going to give you the Holy Spirit through my blood."

Every sermon in the book of Acts is about the death and resurrection of Christ. All of Paul's epistles center on what happened in the death and resurrection of Christ. You can get anything you need from this event. Healing, prosperity, joy, victory — whatever you need — you can get from the fact that, "I was crucified with Christ. He took my place because He was my substitute. He took my condition."

> *For he hath made him to be sin for us, who knew no sin; that we might be made the righteousness of God in him. - 2 Corinthians 5:21*
>
> *...God identified Him with everything in the whole realm of sin.... - Blackwelder*

Everything God did in Christ, He did for you. It is credited to your account just as if you did it. That is why Paul said, "I was there."

LAW FOUR: SAMENESS
OR BEING IDENTICAL

Your identification with Christ is wrapped around an identical identity, which means "sameness, to be the same in all qualities under consideration, or same." You will see this "sameness" over and over again in the scriptures.

> *But if the Spirit of him that raised up Jesus from the dead dwell in you, he that raised up Christ from the dead shall also quicken your mortal bodies by his Spirit that dwelleth in you.*
> *- Romans 8:11*

This reveals that the same identical Spirit dwells in you, and that is your identification. Say this out loud: "I was identified with Christ in His death and resurrection. Right now, I have an identical life and the same spirit, same righteousness, same victory, and same blessing. I was twinned with Christ."

Some would ask, "Does that mean I do not have any personality?" What most people call their personality is really a conglomeration of abuse; i.e., what somebody told them and their identification with their race, their parents, or their employment. You will never really find your true identity or even your true personality until you find out who you are in Christ.

Once you climb up in Him, then God will change your name and tell you who you are. Your mama does not tell you who you are. Your friends at school do not tell you who you are. Your body does not tell you who you are. God says, "I will tell you who you are."

The same Spirit that raised Christ from the dead dwells in us. In the believer is the identical life that raised Christ from the dead. We share the same righteousness and the same victory that is in Christ. If we could see what God sees, we would see that we have the same Spirit that raised Christ. We have the same anointing that was and is on Him. He is the Anointed One, and we are in Him.

God did not give us an inferior product. He gave us the very life of Christ Himself. It is identical! Satan does not want the Church to understand or walk in the reality of our redemption in Christ.

I am crucified with Christ: nevertheless I live; yet not I, but Christ liveth in me: and the life which I now live in the flesh I live by the faith of the Son of God, who loved me, and gave himself for me. - Galatians 2:20

I have been crucified with Christ, and I live now not with my own life but with the life of Christ who lives in me.... - Jerusalem Bible

I have been crucified with Christ. Now it is not my old self, but Christ himself who lives in me.... - Noli

Christ took me to the cross with Him, and I died there with Him.... - Laubach

Yes, I have shared Messiah's crucifixion. I am living indeed, but it is not I that live, it is Messiah whose life is in me....
- Arthur S. Way

I consider myself as having died and now enjoying a second existence, which is simply Jesus using my body. - Distilled Bible

The Apostle Paul's statement in Galatians 2:20 is the clearest statement of every believer's identification with Christ. It is also the simplest understanding of Christianity. Christ the Messiah, the Anointed One, lives in us. I heard T.L. Osborn say, "No other religion can say what the Christian can, that is that our God lives in us." The greatest revelation of the Bible is Christ's identification with us and our identification with Him. He lives in us! Again Paul says in Colossians 1:27, "To whom God would make known what is the riches of the glory of this mystery among the Gentiles; which is Christ in you, the hope of glory." The resurrected Christ, the triumphant Christ, is living in us individually and collectively as the body of Christ. How could you be defeated with Christ, the

Anointed One, living in you? The glory that the first Adam lost is restored in Christ, the last Adam.

Our God did not stay in Heaven; He identified with us, became a man, and embraced our condition so we might live in Him, and He might live in us. The believer's identification with Christ is the glory and the mystery of Christianity.

The Power
of
Identification

5

BEING "IN CHRIST-ED"

Therefore if any man be in Christ, he is a new creature: old things are passed away; behold, all things are become new. - 2 Corinthians 5:17

What does being "in Christ" mean? Some Bible translations simply say "in union with Christ." The Translator's New Testament lists five key phrases: in Christ, in Him, in Whom, in the Lord, or in the Spirit. Actually, those two words "in Christ" (or "in Him" or "in Whom"), are used more than 130 times in the Apostle Paul's letters to tell you who you are in Christ and what you have in Him.

One writer said it this way: "When you are born again or saved, you get 'in Christ-ed.'" What does it mean whatever is in Him is in you. You are in Him or in union with Him. So we will state it this way: You look a whole lot better in Christ than you do outside of Christ.

A BRAND-NEW CREATION

We are studying about the new birth, or being in Christ. 2 Corinthians 5:17 is one of the classic places where Paul uses this phrase: "Therefore if any man be in Christ...." He did not say "be in church." If any man "be in Christ," he is a new creature, or a new creation.

"...Old things are passed away; behold, all things are become new." Really, the first part of verse 18 goes with this verse: "And all things are of God." Other translations just say, "All of these things are of God," or "This is the work of God." God has done this.

In the new birth, you are not just a forgiven sinner. When you get born again, you become a brand-new creation in Christ Jesus. You are recreated.

Often people think the new birth is going from being a lost worm to being a saved worm. In their minds, they still think of themselves as sinners, or as worms struggling to get along, but you have been born of God — "re-fathered" by God or "re-gened." A genetic change has taken place in your spirit. You are a brand-new creation. Old things are passed away; everything is new.

A NEW CREATURE

But God forbid that I should glory, save in the cross of our Lord Jesus Christ, by whom the world is crucified unto me, and I unto the world. For in Christ Jesus neither circumcision availeth anything, nor uncircumcision, but a new creature. - Galatians 6:14,15

Here we have this same phrase again: "a new creature." What is Paul talking about? "Circumcision or uncircumcision is not what matters," he says, "but being a brand-new creature, a brand-new creation 'in Christ,' or being born again."

Let's look back at 2 Corinthians 5:17: "...a brandnew creature." Some translate 2 Corinthians 5:17 this way, "that if any man be in Christ, he is a new creature, a new creation." The words used in the

Greek simply mean "a brand-new species of being." God made a brand-new creation.

You are a brand-new creation in several ways. First, your spirit has been recreated with the very life and nature of God on the inside of you. Second, you are not a Jew, and you are not a Gentile. You are a new nationality; a new species of being. You are in Christ Jesus, so you are blessed with Abraham's blessing, but you are not really a Jew, and you are not really a Gentile. You are a new creation.

Again, look at 2 Corinthians 5:17: "Therefore if any man BE in Christ, he is...." Often we talk about what we are trying to be, needing to be, struggling to be, or going to be someday, but nobody ever told us what we "be." In the new birth we are not talking about what you are trying to be, what you are needing to be, or what you are going to be. We are talking about what you are—every good thing that is in you now. This is something that is already yours the moment you are in Christ Jesus because of the grace of God.

Jesus said, "You shall know the truth, and the truth will make you free" (John 8:32). So you have to know the truth, or you have to have knowledge of good things (plural) that are in you now (not someday, but right now). Good things are in you because you are in Christ.

> *For if anybody is in union with Christ, he is the work of a new creation. The old condition has passed away, a new condition has come....*
> *- 2 Corinthians 5:17, Williams*

> *Therefore if any person is [engrafted] in Christ (the Messiah) he is a new creation (a new creature altogether); the old [previous moral and spiritual condition] has passed away. Behold, the fresh and new has come. - Amplified Bible*

> *Therefore, if anyone is in union with Christ, he is a new being! His old life has passed away and a new life has begun!*
> *- Twentieth Century New Testament*

> *If a man is in Christ, he is created new. The man he was has passed away, and, behold, a new man has been created! - Laubach*

> *When anyone is united to Christ, there is a*
> *new world; the old order has gone, new order*
> *has already begun. - New English Bible*

> *A true Christian is not merely a man altered,*
> *but a man remade.... - Deane*

When you get born again, you have not been repaired or fixed somehow. God has not changed you a little bit. You have not added going to church to your weekly schedule. The moment you get born again, you are in Christ. You have been "in Christ-ed." Whatever is in Him flows into you. You are literally put in union with Christ. How does that happen? Where does that happen? It happens through the miracle of the new birth in your spirit.

"IN CHRIST-ED"

> *For we are his workmanship, created in Christ*
> *Jesus unto good works, which God hath before*
> *ordained that we should walk in them.*
> *- Ephesians 2:10*

(...taking paths which He prepared ahead of time) that we should walk in them — living the good life which He prearranged and made ready for us to live. - Amplified Bible

Some things have been pre-arranged for you. You do not have to worry. God is able to make plans ahead of time and have things in the right place at the right time. He knows what year you will get there, and He knows exactly what you will need when you get there. It will be waiting for you. Once you obey God, then you will see His provision. Once you obey God and follow the path He has for you, you will find He has pre-arranged things for you, just like He did for Abraham when he obeyed God. The ram was in the thicket when Abraham needed it.

And Abraham lifted up his eyes, and looked and behold behind him a ram caught in a thicket by his horns: and Abraham went and took the ram, and offered him up for a burnt offering in the stead of his son. - Genesis 22:13

In Christ, you are the workmanship or the handiwork of God, created in Christ. God does not make any trash, so you could not be trash. You cannot be defeated because God does not make failures. Failures are manmade.

RIGHTEOUS NOW

"For he hath made him to be sin for us, who knew no sin; that we might be made the righteousness of God in him" 2 Corinthians 5:21. Here is another good thing for you to acknowledge: "I have been made the righteousness of God in Christ, I acknowledge that and I confess it." Often people say, "I can never say that I am righteous." People are taught this in religious circles by taking one scripture from the book of Romans out of context: "...There is none righteous, no, not one" Romans 3:10. Actually, this is talking about man's condition in Adam before the death, burial, and resurrection of Christ. Romans 3:23 says, "For all have sinned, and come short of the glory of God." Once you are born again, you are not in Adam; you are in Christ, and this does not apply to you.

If you sin, God has made provision in 1 John 1:9: "If we confess our sins, he is faithful and just to forgive us our sins, and to cleanse us from all unrighteousness." If you are cleansed from all unrighteousness, what happened? You are restored to righteousness!

Now go to Romans 3:24: "Being justified freely by his grace through the redemption that is in Christ Jesus." Right now you are righteous. Romans 3:21 says, "But now the righteousness of God without the law is manifested...." Clinton Utterbach wrote a great song entitled "Righteous Now." I am not trying to be, do not hope to be, I am righteous now in Christ Jesus.

Righteousness is a gift according to Romans 5:17. You will never be any more righteous than you are right now. You cannot grow in righteousness. You can grow in sanctification and holiness, but righteousness is a free gift.

DRESSED UP IN CHRIST

In Christ, you have been made righteous. You need to acknowledge that. This is all a part of "putting on" the new man. (I discuss this more in Chapter 13). By dressing up, you are not still wearing the same old clothes and smelling the same way. You do not wear the shame, guilt, or oppression anymore when you get dressed up in the righteousness of God. You have robes of righteousness that you put on every day. One way to put them on is through your confession and declaration according to Philemon 6. Renew your mind with the Word of God, and begin to declare your righteousness in Christ by saying, "I am the righteousness of God in Christ."

BLESSED IN CHRIST

Blessed be the God and Father of our Lord Jesus Christ, who hath blessed us with all spiritual blessings in heavenly places in Christ.
- Ephesians 1:3

He has blessed us. We are blessed with every spiritual blessing in heavenly places in Christ. We are seated in heavenly places. We are blessed with the same blessings Jesus has right now in the presence of God. We have the blessing of the Lord upon our lives. Every blessing that Heaven itself enjoys is ours right now. We do not have to wait until we get to Heaven. In Christ, we already have those blessings. We are already blessed with the same life, righteousness, joy, peace, and love. We can climb up in that rock of who we are in Christ and get up there in the glory of Heaven!

VICTORY IN CHRIST

Now thanks be unto God, which always causeth us to triumph in Christ, and maketh manifest the savour of his knowledge by us in every place.
- 2 Corinthians 2:14

Everywhere you go, the triumph and the smell of victory on you is greater than whatever is around you. The triumph of Christ in you and the smell of that triumph comes out of you and has an effect on the atmosphere wherever you go.

FREE IN CHRIST

There is therefore now no condemnation to them which are in Christ Jesus, who walk not after the flesh, but after the Spirit. For the law of the Spirit of life in Christ Jesus hath made me free from the law of sin and death.
- Romans 8:1,2

One translation says, "There is no sentence of guilt against those who are in Christ." You are not guilty anymore. The devil is the accuser of the brethren. If

Satan can get you under condemnation, he can cheat you out of your inheritance in Christ. You can see why it is important to have a righteousness consciousness, or to dress up in righteousness.

BOLDNESS IN CHRIST

"In whom we have boldness and access with confidence by the faith of him," Ephesians 3:12. This is one of my favorite scriptures. You get some boldness when you get in Him. God does not want you dragging in, crawling in, or sliding into His presence. He wants you to come walking in like a child of God. You have a "standing" with God that the angels do not have. God wants you to come walking in saying, "Abba Father, Daddy God, you are my Father, and I am your child. I have access with boldness, confidence, and assurance into your presence."

I know God is glad to see me when I enter His presence. Numbers 23:21 says, "He hath not beheld iniquity in Jacob, neither hath he seen perverseness in Israel...." When you come walking into His presence in Christ and through the blood of Jesus, God cannot find anything wrong with you — not even a trace of sin. It is as if you had never sinned. You are justified in Christ.

Righteousness gives you boldness in your prayer life. In Him, you have boldness when you pray. You are not a beggar; you come into God's presence with confidence saying, "I am an heir of God and a joint-heir with Jesus Christ. Father God, I know when I pray, I have this confidence, that whatever I ask for, You hear me, and I know I have the petitions I desire of You." We get boldness in the presence of God. Where do we get it? "IN WHOM we have boldness and access with confidence in His presence," Ephesians 3:12. I have access, or a way into the presence of God in Him. You say, "What is the way in?" You must climb up in Christ by faith declaring, "I am in Him."

MADE READY IN CHRIST

"Giving thanks unto the Father, which hath made us meet to be partakers of the inheritance of the saints in light," Colossians 1:12. The word "meet" in the King James Version just simply means that God has qualified us, enabled us, made us worthy, or made us ready. You will never be more ready for your inheritance than the moment you receive Jesus Christ as your Lord and Savior.

In other words, you do not have to sing in the choir for 38 years to be ready. The moment you are washed in the blood of Jesus — the moment you climb in Christ by faith and receive Him as your Lord and Savior — you are qualified for your inheritance. You do not have to do anything else. You just got "in Christ-ed."

Colossians 1:12 says, "Giving thanks unto the Father...." Sometimes you need to say, "O, Father, I give You thanks that You have qualified me. You have enabled me and made me worthy."

There is a time when we bow down before God in reverence and in worship, but that is not being unworthy. When we come into the presence of God by the blood of Jesus and bow down, there are times when God will say, "Stand up with boldness and declare that you are who I say you are." It gives Him honor when you believe Him.

WISDOM IN CHRIST

"In whom are hid all the treasures of wisdom and knowledge," Colossians 2:3. The treasures of wisdom and knowledge in Him are hidden or stored up just for you. They are not hidden from you; they are hidden for you. In other words, God is not going to take all these wonderful things and lay them out in the street.

God has a secret place where He has hidden them for people who receive Jesus. You have access into the secret place where all are stored. Whatever knowledge, direction, understanding, or wisdom you need for your children, your finances, or your future is stored up in Christ.

The Good News Bible says, "He is the key that opens all the hidden treasures of God's wisdom and knowledge." Wisdom and knowledge are more valuable than money. If you get the money with no wisdom, you won't keep the money long, but if you get wisdom, you can get money no matter what happens or where you go. They can take your clothing, your house, and your car, but if you have wisdom, you will get it all back.

PATIENT IN CHRIST

Someone said, "Not only is the devil stupid; he is also impatient." God is patient, which is one of the fruits of the Spirit. He has the time and space

for things to happen. The Bible says, "...through faith
and patience inherit the promises," Hebrews 6:12.
The devil will hang around and try to whip you, but
finally he will get impatient and say, "I guess this is
not going to work," and he will take off. You can
outlast the devil!

Sometime ago when I visited someone at a
hospital, I needed to ride the elevator to get to their
floor. So I punched the button for the elevator to come
and the light came on. I waited and waited for the
doors to open. Finally, I punched the button again
even though the light was still on. I thought, "I guess
I don't need to punch it again. The light is on. It is on
the way." I could have been impatient and taken the
stairs if I wanted, but I held steady.

When you exercise your faith, you have punched
the button, and the light is on. The devil will say, "It
is not going to come. It will never happen." Keep the
switch of faith turned on. Keep that light on. Every
morning when you get up, say, "The light is on. My
faith is still working. Miracles are coming to me. The
elevator is on the way." You will not have to carry your
miracle; your miracle will carry you.

Although the devil has some knowledge, he had to
be stupid to run out on God. He is so stupid, he still

thinks he has some time and he is going to win. Did you know you could start shouting praises to God, and your enemies will start attacking each other? As a matter of fact, the Old Testament says that when the people started praising Him, God caused the enemy to turn and attack itself.

FREE FROM SIN IN CHRIST

One time a minister friend of mine had a vision in which he saw demonic activity in the realm of the Spirit. He said, "I saw demons flying like a bunch of dumb chicken hawks." You could say that sin makes you stupid. There is no "smart" sin because sin is rebellion against God and aligning yourself with the devil. Sin is self-destructive and stupid.

The television program "America's Dumbest Criminals" is hilarious. They show actual video footage and policemen tell stories of the stupid things criminals do. One program showed some men robbing a convenience store. After they robbed the store, they drove off in their van that had a "For Sale" sign in the back window with a phone number on it. The clerk saw the phone number in the van and gave the police the number!

The police called it and said, "We would like to know if you have a van for sale." The robbers said, "We sure do." The police said, "We would like to buy it. Could you bring it over?" The robbers took the van over, and the police arrested them. Sin makes you stupid.

They showed another man holding a gun on the clerk behind the counter. The clerk got so nervous, he could not open the cash register, so the criminal put the gun down to help open it. The man running the cash register grabbed the gun and pointed it at the criminal who ran out of the store.

The dumbest thing that the devil tells you is that you will never get caught. The devil is a liar and a deceiver. When people get caught and then get out of prison, the devil says, "Next time, you won't get caught." So they do something else that is stupid and end up in prison again. Why does this happen? Sin makes you stupid. The devil wants to destroy you. He wants you to look stupid and to miss out on the blessings of God.

In Christ, the wisdom, knowledge, and understanding of God help you miss the traps and pitfalls of the devil and walk in the goodness and prearranged things of God. Anytime someone suggests you do something that is a crime, just say, "Hey, I am not going to be stupid." When the devil tries to get you to sin, say, "No, I am not stupid."

RIGHT RELATIONSHIPS IN CHRIST

In Christ, we have access to the understanding and the insight of God. We have access to the laws and principles of God and the abundance of God. Sometimes your relationships can be all messed up because you never had any insight. The Holy Spirit gives you access to everything that is in Christ, and He will warn you about wrong relationships.

Dad Hagin said, "Any person who shuts his spirit away and refuses to develop it will end up being a cripple in life and a victim of scheming and designing people." In Christ, we have access to the understanding and insight of God.

Gambling casinos are built on losers, not winners. If somebody does win, he still ultimately loses because he will stay there until he loses what he has won. When I was preaching in Las Vegas, I was riding in the hotel elevator and a man asked me if I was winning or losing. I said, "I'm winning! They don't have any of my money. Ha, ha, ha!"

In Christ are all the treasures of wisdom and knowledge. God will put you in right relationships where people are not out to manipulate or hurt you. You are then in a double-win situation. They are in Christ, and they say, "I am rooting for you to win because when you win, I win. I want you to win and have God's plan and purpose for your life."

COMPLETE IN HIM

For in him dwelleth all the fullness of the Godhead bodily. And ye are complete in him, which is the head of all principality and power.
- Colossians 2:9,10

[And I pray] that the participation in and sharing of your faith may produce and promote full recognition and appreciation and understanding and precise knowledge of every good [thing] that is ours in [our identification with] Christ Jesus [and unto His glory].
- Philemon 6, Amplified

We are complete in Christ. As believers we need to meditate on every good thing that is in Christ. Think about them and say them out loud. Acknowledge and declare every good thing that is in Him because when you are in Him, they are in you.

Look up the scriptures on your identification with Christ. Look up the scriptures on substitution. Everything Jesus did was for you. After you see what He has done for you, then declare what He has done for you. Declare your identity in Him and who you are in Him. You are a new creation in Him, righteous in Him, blessed in Him, forgiven in Him, redeemed in Him, and complete in Him!

6

IN CHRIST
APPLICATIONS

Recently, I was shopping for a new cell phone and my son informed me about an iPhone that would move me into hi-tech communications. I told him that all I wanted was a phone that would make and receive calls. Then my secretary joined in, telling me how it would make communication much better. Then my daughter joined in. Seeing how I was outnumbered, I gave in and became the owner of an iPhone! Soon, we were all exploring all the possibilities available to us with this new phone and were jokingly considering going to school to learn about it!

When I first turned the phone on, there were all kinds of pictures, I couldn't even figure out how to make a phone call. I later learned that each picture was an application that would perform a different function on this new phone. With one touch I can open various functions such as the calendar, the weather anywhere in the world, a calculator, a clock, the stock market (not recommended for those struggling with depression), e-mail, the internet, or the Holy Bible in 21 translations. I can also access the yellow pages, use it for a dictionary, or I can find a fitness gym anywhere in the United States (you can tell I'm into physical fitness). I get up every morning, run around the block four times, push the block back under the bed and go back to sleep! I could read the newspaper, watch CBS Sports, Skype, find a Fed-Ex anywhere, or find a restaurants or Starbucks in any city. I have found the endless applications on this phone absolutely amazing, but remember before I got the iPhone, all I wanted was a phone!

My son Aaron said, "Dad, you're really going to like this button." He explained the one marked "App Store" would give me access to all the applications or functions of the iPhone. I began to see with this particular technology, more possibilities were available to me than I had ever taken advantage of before.

The Holy Spirit spoke up in my spirit and said, "That is like many Christians who go to church and say, 'All I want is to go to Heaven when I die.'" Yes, it's true, you can be born again and you can receive eternal life, but there is so much more! With the iPhone, there are over 500,000 applications in the "App Store." In Christ there are endless applications! The Holy Spirit has been sent to teach us about the "App Store" or all the applications of who the believer is "in Christ." There are at least 130 in Christ scriptures that open endless possibilities for believers to access! The treasures of wisdom and knowledge are stored up in Christ, waiting for any believer to enter in. You can open blessings, your inheritance, wisdom, strength, healing, provision, power, counsel and personal victory in every area of life. These applications are very accessible to believer through faith in the blood of Jesus and His Word. The two words "in Christ" give you access to all that is available as you acknowledge who you are and what you have in Christ.

OUR TEACHER, THE HOLY SPIRIT

We have a personal instructor, the Holy Spirit, who is available to guide us in how to open what is ready and waiting for us to enjoy. In the Greek language the Holy Spirit is called the Parakletos. A paraclete is an attorney, counsel for the defense, one called alongside to help. The Paraclete has three areas of expertise: exceptional knowledge, excellence in procedure and protocol and persuasive speaking ability. Oh, what a comfort the Holy Spirit is in times of need and great trial. What a companion to walk through life with. Oh, what a teacher of the language of faith and redemption!

And I will pray the Father, and he shall give you another Comforter, that he may abide with you forever; Even the Spirit of truth; whom the world cannot receive, because it seeth him not, neither knoweth him: but ye know him; for he dwelleth with you, and shall be in you. At that day ye shall know that I am in my Father, and ye in me, and I in you. - John 14:16,17,20

...He [the Spirit] will take the things that are Mine and will reveal (declare, disclose, transmit) it to you. - John 16:15, Amplified

Jesus said that when the Holy Spirit, our Paraclete or Comforter comes, that He would lead us into Truth. He will take the things of Christ and show them, transmit and communicate them to us. Today the Holy Spirit is working in the church revealing what God has done for us in His redemptive work in Christ and helping translate it into our personal victory.

The Holy Spirit wants to lead you into the "App Store" of who you are in Christ and open up the unlimited power, wisdom and precise knowledge of God. The Holy Spirit connects you to all of Heaven's authority so that when you pray and come in contact with any problem it must change. He will think through your mind, speak through your voice, give you a song in the night, and lead you every step of the way!

The Paraclete will help you know when and what to speak! You would not hire an attorney who is "dumber" than you or that had a speech impediment. We desperately need the expertise of the Holy Spirit to know how to pray and what to say because everything in the kingdom of God is activated by believing and speaking. If you listen to the Holy Spirit, He will prompt you to speak the Word of God and who you are in Christ.

The Holy Spirit will prompt you to say words that come from Heaven which will activate great and mighty things in the earth. He has come to help you apply Christ's redemptive work into your personal victory and change the world around you. It is through His power that greater works can be done and the glory of Heaven will fill every part of our lives.

IS YOUR FAITH CONTAGIOUS?

I pray that everyone who meets you may catch your faith and learn from you how wonderful it is to live in Christ. - Philemon 6, Laubach

Paul desires our Christian lives to be effective and contagious so that everyone around us catches what we have. We need to have a full blown case of the victorious life of Christ! Trina and I have eight grandchildren. Our little grandchildren have attended the nurseries in churches where there is a strict rule against admitting children who have a communicative sickness. Certain symptoms will be present if the child has been infected with a virus or cold and it is in a communicative form. If the child is allowed into an area where other children are, there is a strong probability of others catching the same thing. In the same way there are certain symptoms present when a Christian's faith is in what we call a communicative form.

Notice the two words "in Christ." There are certain symptoms that show up when you are a contagious Christian! The symptoms that show up when Christ is in you are evident to those around you. Those symptoms include confidence, joy, love, hope and peace. "The communication of thy faith may become effectual by the acknowledging of every good thing which is in you in Christ," Philemon 6. The Amplified Bible says we can effectually share our faith by "...full recognition and appreciation and understanding and precise knowledge of every good thing that is ours in our identification with Christ Jesus."

When people get around you, they begin to catch what you have which comes from being in close contact and union with Christ. The same life Heaven is enjoying right now is overflowing in you and everyone you meet can tell you've been with Jesus. You become infectious and a carrier of His divine life. You can't help but share your faith, lay hands on the sick, love people and be a giver. You have the answer and when you come into the room things brighten up with joy! How did you get that way? By acknowledging every good thing which is in you because you are in union with Jesus. Watch out! Someone is about to catch what you have!

APPLICATION OF THE BLOOD

Before the children of Israel could leave Egypt, the blood of a spotless lamb had to be applied to the doorposts of each home. The way the blood was applied was with the hyssop branch. In Exodus 12, that blood preserved the people who applied it from the death angel. It delivered them from slavery and brought the nation of Israel out with strength and great wealth. Today the blood of Jesus is applied to our lives by the "hyssop" of our tongue or our personal confession of faith in it. It is not mere knowledge of the redeeming power of the blood of Jesus, but we must have a personal revelation of it and act upon it! God said, "When I see the Blood, I will pass over you." What a powerful application which grants us access to the Throne of God, protection from every evil work and power to overcome everything which may stand in your way.

In every situation, every step of the way, the Holy Spirit is guiding us to apply all God has provided for every believer to live a blessed and victorious life! He has provided all we need to do His will. Now thanks be unto God which always causes us to triumph in Christ!"

7

GOD'S GENETIC ENGINEERING

The scientific world got upset because in England they were reportedly able to produce genetically identical sheep by cloning. The word "clone" simply means "the technique of producing a genetically identical duplicate, genetic engineering." If anyone could be involved in genetic engineering, it would have to be the Creator.

"Therefore if any man be in Christ, he is a new creature: old things are passed away; behold, all things are become new," 2 Corinthians 5:17. What God has done is put a new gene in you! You have been regenerated. God connected your genetic structure to the Lord Jesus Christ. The same qualities He put in Christ, He put in you.

Three things determine what you are and your potential in life. One of them is genetic determinism, which means your parents made you what you are. Genetic determinism says that your problem is in your genes. However, if you have been born again, you have a whole new genetic structure. You have some DNA from Jesus! Even your molecular structure and your blood were changed. Your spirit or your inner man was changed, and you are not the same anymore.

GENETICALLY CHANGED

When I was a teenager, an evangelist friend of mine came out of the Jesus People Movement and started preaching. When he was a teenager, he was put in prison. While there, he surrendered his life to Jesus and was born again.

The only evidence the police had against him was some of his hair. When his case came to trial, the prosecutor could not use that evidence because after he had been born again, the structure of his body and his hair was genetically changed. He was a totally different person. His DNA was different from the person who had committed the crime. They could not convict him because he was not the same man! He knew it was because he had been born again. He said, "I am not the same man." He was released because he had a different identity.

Did you know that when you get born again, you get identified with Christ? You are not kind of getting saved or someday going to Heaven, but your spirit literally has brand new DNA. Genetically you are changed. You are joined to Christ with the same life, power, righteousness, glory, Spirit, and qualities He has. This gets in your spirit and changes your blood cells, your destiny, your future, and everything about you.

You are not the same anymore. You cannot be the same, so do not let the devil tell you that you have not changed and you are the same person. No, if any man be in Christ, he is a new creation. Old things are passed away, and everything has become new.

When you get born again, the devil has no evidence against you. He tries to bring his evidence before the throne of God and say, "I have proof that this person did this and that." God says, "Let's check the DNA. No, that is not the same person. That person is dead and gone." You literally are a brand-new creation in Christ Jesus.

A CHOSEN GENERATION

But you are a chosen generation, a royal priesthood, an holy nation, a peculiar people; that ye should shew forth the praises of him who hath called you out of darkness into his marvelous light. - 1 Peter 2:9

When you get born again, you get regenerated. The word "regenerated" and the word "gene" come from the same root word. In other words, you get re-gened. You get new DNA. There is a champion in your genetic line. His name is Jesus. He passed on that champion, thoroughbred bloodline, to you. If you have mule in your bloodline, you will never be a racehorse, but if you can trace your lineage back to the champion, you can say, "I am not a mule. I am a racehorse. I am a thoroughbred. I have been re-bred by God."

1 Peter 2:9 says, "You are a chosen generation...." The word "generation" and the word "regenerated" have the same root word. Your genetic makeup no longer comes from Adam or your past. It comes from Almighty God and the same qualities that are in Christ are in you. You have some DNA in your inner man or your spirit man that came from God.

Even though you are born again, the devil will do everything he can to keep you from walking in the light of who you are in Christ. The key is to declare continually who you are in Christ. Let the Holy Spirit continually bring this to bear upon your natural influences.

Do you have any natural influences? Your emotions, your soul, your past, your anger, your temper, your poverty, and your habits say, "Oh, that's just the way I am." But when you know who you are in Christ, your spirit man rises up and says, "That is not the way I am. I am in Christ. I am redeemed. I am righteous. I am saved. I am triumphant. I am blessed. I am healed. I have been born of God."

The Apostle Peter is talking about getting regenerated. You are a chosen generation. You are getting re-gened. You can say, "I have some new genes, and I am going to wear my new genes."

A ROYAL PRIESTHOOD

"But you are a chosen generation, a royal priesthood...." Other translations say, "You are a priesthood." You do not have to go to the priest anymore; you are a priest. Look in the mirror. In the Old Testament everyone had to go to the priest. In the New Testament, because of what God has done for us in Christ, you are in a whole new creation where everyone is a priest. What does that mean?

Everyone from the greatest to the least has equal access to the Father God. I do not have any more access to God than you do. You have just as much access as I do. God is just as glad to see you as He is to see any preacher, apostle, or prophet. You can go right into the presence of God. You are a royal priesthood.

In other words, your inner man, your spirit, is granted access into the very presence of God. You are a royal priesthood. The Weymouth translation says, "A priesthood of kingly lineage." You need to find out where you came from — you came from the King.

When you were born again, you walked out of Adam, and you walked into Christ. You got "in Christ-ed" and you are royalty. I have traced my lineage now, and I am of royalty. 1 Peter 2:9 says, "You are a chosen generation, a royal priesthood, an holy nation, a peculiar people...." I have a new nationality. I am a chosen generation.

Let's finish reading this: "...an holy nation...." He called the Church a nation. Once you get in Christ, that is your only nationality. That does not mean I am not proud to be an American, but you have to understand, I have family all over the world. I have a new citizenship. Once you get in this nation, you are granted citizenship, and all the military will back you up. There are all kinds of benefits.

A PECULIAR PEOPLE

"...A peculiar people...," he says. What makes you so peculiar? While the world's economy may be going down, yours is going up. When everyone else is depressed, you are shouting and jumping. Now that is peculiar. "...that ye should shew forth the praises of him who hath called you out of darkness into his marvelous light." The Jordan translation says, "...you are a show stock people."

What does "show stock" mean? God wants the world to look at this new breed. It is not black, it is not white, it is not Hispanic, and it is not Asian. This new breed is a whole new nation, a whole new creation. You say, "What is it?" The answer to racism is not religion; the answer to racism is "in Christ."

God wants to put you in a show and say, "Hey, look at these fat calves over here. I have them well-groomed, and they do not have the mange." We are not talking about a mangy, half-dead old cow with a broken leg. We are talking about show stock.

Have you ever been to a livestock show? I went to a big rodeo in El Paso, Texas, to see all the show stock. When they brought out those cows, sheep, and other animals, they were well-groomed and looked really good. God wants the church to walk out blessed and strong, full of joy, peace, and victory. He wants to bring you out and say, "This is the way I treat my people."

FORMER NOBODIES

1 Peter 2:10 says, "Which in time past were not a people...." There has never been a people or a nation like this nation. "But are the people of God: which had not obtained mercy, but now have obtained mercy."

Another translation says it this way, "...the former nobodies are now God's somebodies." Have you ever been around people that ignore you as if you are nobody? Doesn't that irritate you?

Who this world says is somebody is really nobody in the light of eternity. People will stand around in hotels in Las Vegas and wait for somebody. When a movie star walks into a church, everyone will be buzzing, "Do you know who was in church last night?" Instead, you ought to look around and say, "Do you know who was in church last night? We had a lot of somebodies."

Because you are in Christ, you cannot be a nobody. When you are in Christ, you have access to the highest place in the universe. You can go right to the throne of God and say, "Abba Father. That is my daddy. I get immediate recognition. I am well known in the realm of the Spirit."

In Acts 19:13-16 when the seven sons of Sceva tried to cast that devil out, he said, "Jesus I know and Paul I know, but who are you?" Do you need to find out who you are? You cannot tell the devil, "My pastor said...." The devil will say, "I know Jesus, and I know your pastor, but who are you?"

You have a reputation not only in Heaven, but also in hell. Your picture is up on the wall of the post office in hell with the caption, "Kill this person. Stop him any way you can."

When you know the Greater One lives on the inside of you, and you have been born of God, you know the devil does not have a shot at you. Whenever he comes around, you always disappear! You climb right up into Christ.

The devil says, "Where did he go?" You look just like Christ because the anointing of Christ comes on you. Climb up into the rock Moses climbed into. He received a revelation of God and saw the glory of God. You can, too.

You are somebody in Christ. The reason people kill themselves is because they think, "I am not anybody. Nobody cares about me. I walk by people, and they do not even look at me." They get an inferiority complex.

One man said, "I didn't have any complex; I really was inferior!" However, most people are not really inferior. The devil has lied to them so long, they believe what he has told them, and then they go through life believing they are inferior.

When you know who you are in Christ, you cannot have an inferiority complex. I am not talking about being arrogant; I am talking about a simple, calm assurance of what God has done for you in Christ and who you are in Him.

THINGS ARE ARRANGED
AHEAD FOR YOU

You are *somebody* in Him. When somebody important like the President of the United States goes somewhere, arrangements are made ahead of time for him. Important people do not show up and then people start jumping around trying to fix something for them.

When you are a *somebody* in Christ, God has things prearranged ahead of time for you. Walking by faith and not by sight causes things to be set up ahead of time because *somebody* is coming.

When you are in a hospital room and the doctor tells you that the person in that room is going to die, you say, "Hold it! *Somebody* just walked in. I have authority in the name of Jesus to lay hands on the sick, and they shall recover." You cannot judge or estimate yourself after the flesh. You have to see yourself in Christ.

CONNECTED WITH CHRIST

I am crucified with Christ: nevertheless I live; yet not I, but Christ liveth in me: and the life which I now live in the flesh I live by the faith of the Son of God, who loved me, and gave himself for me. - Galatians 2:20

Our identification is revealed in the beginning of Galatians 2:20. The King James Version uses "I am" to connect the believer's crucifixion directly to Christ's crucifixion. Every other translation of Galatians 2:20 uses the past tense: "I was" or "I have been."

I have been crucified with Christ. Now it is not my old self but Christ himself who lives in me. - Noli

I have been crucified with Christ, and I live now not with my own life but with the life of Christ who lives in me. - Jerusalem Bible

Christ took me to the cross with Him, and I died there with Him. - Laubach

Yes, I have shared Messiah's crucifixion. I am living indeed, but it is not I that live, it is Messiah or Christ whose life is in me. - Arthur S. Way

I have been crucified with Christ. My own life is dead; it is Christ who lives in me. True, my

*physical life goes on, but its main spring is faith
in the Son of God. - Barclay*

*I consider myself as having died and now
enjoying a second existence, which is simply
Jesus using my body. - Distilled Bible*

Here the Apostle Paul is talking about our
identification with Christ. The center of our redemption
is what God did for us in Christ, or our identification
with Christ. There are several other scriptures that
form the foundation of identification with Christ.

FREE FROM SIN

*Knowing this, that our old man is crucified with
him, that the body of sin might be destroyed,
that henceforth we should not serve sin.
- Romans 6:6*

The King James Version says, "...my old man IS
crucified with him." Every other translation in the
Greek uses the past tense. My old man is crucified
with Him for what purpose? "...that the body of sin
might be destroyed, that henceforth, I should not serve

sin," so I could be free from the dominion and the control of sin. We know from Romans 6:6 that our old man is, was, and has been crucified with Christ.

One important thing needs to be emphasized again. What Paul is talking about in Galatians 2:20 is not a spiritual state you will grow into one day. I have heard preachers say, "Someday, I want to be able to say with the Apostle Paul, 'I was crucified with Christ: nevertheless I live; yet not I, but Christ lives in me.'" In other words, their concept of Galatians 2:20 is that Paul is talking about a spiritual state he had attained after thirty years of serving God.

Actually, Paul is talking about revelation knowledge of what happened in the death, burial, and resurrection of Christ. This is true for every person, and specifically true for every believer the moment you accept Jesus Christ as your Lord and Savior. You do not need to grow in spiritual maturity for thirty years. The moment you accept Jesus, you have a whole new identity that is tied up with what happened in the death, burial, and resurrection of Christ.

This is not a spiritual state you are attaining; it is something God did for you in Christ. It is an absolute fact that you can say Galatians 2:20 is talking about you right now, today. You do not need to wait until you have thirty years of spiritual maturity before you can apply this verse to yourself.

OUR OLD MAN WAS CRUCIFIED WITH HIM

We can see from Romans 6:6 that it would not be a case of spiritual maturity. Galatians 2:20 could not be a case of spiritual progression, or you could not connect it to Romans 6:6 because it says, "...our old man is [or was] crucified with him." When you say "old man," who are you talking about? "Old man" is simply your old self.

Other translations say, "The person that I used to be," "My former unregenerate self," or "My old sinful self, my former self." One of my favorite translations says, "My former evil identity." My former evil identity was crucified with Him. My old rebel self which was always rebelling against God was exterminated.

Another translation says, "My old inherited self." In other words, what runs in your family does not run in you anymore. You get certain characteristics from birth. Your old man really is Adam, who you are in Adam, and Adam's impact upon your life. Your first birth puts you in Adam, but your second birth puts you in Christ. In Adam, you shared his inheritance, condition, and future. In Christ, you share His inheritance, His condition, and His future.

Are you in Christ? When you were born again, you got out of the old man Adam and into the new man Christ. Whatever was passed on to you genetically is gone, and now you have a new genetic structure. No trace — not even a molecule — is left of what you used to be.

A DIFFERENT PERSON

Therefore if any man be in Christ, he is a new creature: old things are passed away; behold, all things are become new. - 2 Corinthians 5:17

My old man was crucified with Christ. Romans 6:6 is connected to 2 Corinthians 5:17. Other translations from the Greek say, "a new species of being." You are not just a forgiven sinner. You are not just a changed person. You are a different person.

I do believe in changing after you are born again, but you are not just a changed person with a few things added to you. You are a different person from what you were. Old things are passed away, and everything has become new. The very next phrase of 2 Corinthians 5:18 says, "This is the work of God."

Remember, God is the original "people person." He "manufactures" people. He has the factory and the copyright. No one has ever learned how to make people. If there is a problem with people, He remakes them. God had a problem with the first condition of humanity, so He made a brand-new humanity — a whole new race, a whole new creation.

In Christ, you are not just a forgiven sinner. In Christ, you are a brand-new creation. Old things are passed away. The Amplified Bible says, "... the old [previous moral and spiritual condition] has passed away. Behold, the fresh and new has come!" Everything has become new. This is the work of God.

We can see God throughout the Old and New Testaments literally changing people's identities. Once you see who you are in Christ, you can no longer identify with the old person you used to be. The devil will try to come around and say some things, but the old person you used to be is dead and gone.

YOUR SPIRIT TAKES OVER

There is the putting on of the "new man," which involves renewing the mind and learning to walk in the spirit, but here we are talking about exactly what happened when you were born again. Being in Christ happens in your spirit. You were identified with Christ in His death, burial, and resurrection.

1 Corinthians 6:17 reveals what we call "union with Christ." "But he that is joined unto the Lord is one spirit." When you get born again, your spirit is joined to Christ. When you pray in the Spirit, or you get where the Spirit of God is moving, you want to jump, run, laugh, and do all kinds of things because your spirit is joined to the triumph of Christ. Sometimes your head cannot figure out why you are jumping and running, but you get so full of the Holy Spirit that you see who you are in Christ.

The actual experience of it begins to work out from your spirit, and you start laughing. You are blessed in Him. You are redeemed in Him. You are righteous in Him. You are forgiven in Him. You are triumphant in Him. You are strong in Him. You are prosperous in Him.

Your spirit rises up and begins to take ascendancy over your mind, your reasoning, and your flesh. Your spirit starts acting like who you really are. This is what happens in a Holy Spirit meeting. The Holy Spirit begins to infuse strength into your spirit — your inner man. The Holy Spirit brings out the reality of redemption.

Sometimes people, even born-again Spirit-filled Christians, have been dominated by their flesh and their natural minds so long, they never experience the reality of their redemption in Christ, the reality of their triumph in Christ, and the reality of the blessings that belong to them in Christ.

They do not get much of the reality of it because it is just theology to them. As a matter of fact, when you quote the scripture to them, they say, "Don't quote that scripture to me. I know that scripture. I can quote it to you." Yet they still have the same problem that they have always had. They never get into the reality of redemption.

8

IN CHRIST
DETERMINISM

If you have studied psychology, you know three factors have determined what kind of person you are: genetic determinism, psychic determinism, and environmental determinism. The reason it is called "determinism" is because there is no escape.

There is some truth to all these things, but God brings another factor to believers, which I call "in Christ" determinism. "...if any man be IN CHRIST, he is a new creature: old things are passed away; behold all things are become new," 2 Corinthians 5:17.

Genetic determinism means you are what you are because of your genes. You are what you are because of your parents or what runs in your family. Being in Christ has given you a gene change. That means you have been regenerated or "re-gened." God has done some genetic engineering "in Christ." You have been born of God. God is your Father, Jesus is your older brother, and some new things run in your family.

Psychic determinism means that your identity, your behavior, and your potential are produced by your thinking. Although there is some truth to that, you have some new thoughts now. God said, "I will give you My thoughts now, so have another determinism."

A friend of mine said, that he carries his brains in his hand. When someone asks him what he thinks, he says, "Hold it just a second, let me look in my brains." Then he opens his Bible!

When someone asks you what you think about something, say, "Hold it just a minute. I have my brains right here. Let me see what I think. I think I am healed. I think I am happy. I think I am prosperous. I think my steps are ordered by the Lord. That is what I think."

Environmental determinism means you are what you are, and your surroundings and the influences around you limit your future. Once you are in Christ and in the body of Christ, there are supernatural connections all around you. When you go to your company (your church) and start praying, you are in a whole new environment (Acts 4:23).

What makes you the way that you are? Once you get born again, these three determinism factors all change. Your future and your potential are radically altered as a result of it.

A person with "in Christ" determinism thinks God's thoughts and sees himself in Him. "In Christ" determinism is stronger than any other factor that tries to shape you. There are 130 in Christ, in Him, in Whom, and in the Lord scriptures that show your new identity.

Now look at the last part of 2 Corinthians 5:17, "...old things are passed away; behold, all things are become new." In Christ, old things are passed away. The Wade translation says, "...the original conditions have passed away...they have been replaced by new conditions." The old conditions are gone, and there are new conditions. Everything has become new.

It is good news that all things are made new, but it is also good news that old things are passed away. If all you have as a Christian is something new added to you, you would still have to deal with and live with the old conditions. In Christ old things are passed away. Another translation says, "...dead and gone." Your past is dead and gone.

The Deane translation says, "...a true Christian is not merely a man altered but a man remade." He told Jeremiah, "Go down to the potter's house, and I'll show you how I can take a vessel that has been marred and make it all over again" (Jeremiah 18:4). People will look at you and say, "You don't look like the same person." You can say, "I'm not. I am in Christ."

IDENTIFY WITH CHRIST

People often talk about what happened to them in their past. Their identity and identification are so hooked up with their past, some people even call themselves by an experience that happened to them, such as, "I am divorced." No, divorce might have happened to you, but you are not presently divorced.

Some people identify with what has happened to them. They say, "I was abused." Some people identify with an addiction. They might say, "I am an alcoholic." Then they join a support group and their identity gets worse because everybody there is an alcoholic.

However, your identification with Christ changes

everything. It does not mean that you were not abused, you did not have a problem with drinking, or you were not divorced. People go through all those things, but your identification with Christ is stronger than that. You could say that what happened to you in Christ is bigger than anything else that has happened to you.

This does not mean your past experience did not happen. The devil is mean, and bad things happen to good people. Sometimes things happen to people when they are children and they never get over it. As a matter of fact, when you start talking to people, what happened when they were 12, 15, or 25 years old will come out of their mouths. Even when they are 70 years old, they still talk about what happened. Someone did something to them that impacted their lives so greatly, they never got beyond it.

Oh, but in Christ! What happened to Christ in His death, burial, and resurrection is greater than anything else that ever happened to you. Hallelujah!

POWERFUL PREPOSITIONS

These important prepositions help us understand our identification with Christ: "for," "with," "in," "by," and "through." Arthur S. Way commented in his translation of The Letters of Saint Paul:

> *Prepositions "on," "by," "through," "with"*
> *are compelled frequently to do duty for which*
> *they are inadequate. What they are intended to*
> *express is practically nullified by the fact that*
> *they are required to express too much.*

Therefore, in Paul's epistles they go unnoticed, even though they are the connecting words that show the relationship of the subjects mentioned, in this case the believer's identification with Christ. I agree with Arthur S. Way, and I also would add the preposition "in," which is used more than 130 times in Paul's letters.

The preposition "for" shows substitution. Christ died "for" us or in our behalf. The preposition "with" shows identification. The preposition "in" shows union with Christ. The preposition "through" shows application. For example: "I can do all things through Christ who strengtheneth me" (Philippians 4:13).

The phrase "in Christ" is never translated to mean anything else except "in union with Christ." That is the only other way it can be translated. What does it mean to be "in Christ"?

JOINED TO CHRIST

1 Corinthians 6:17 says, "But he that is joined unto the Lord is one spirit." What does that mean? When you were born again, your spirit was joined to the Master, or joined to Christ. Like a bay of water is one with the ocean, your spirit is one with Christ. When the water rises in the ocean, it rises in the bay. The same stuff that is in the ocean gets into the bay. The same stuff that is in Christ right now is in you. I am talking about the same stuff — the same life, same victory, same joy, and same power.

ACKNOWLEDGE YOUR UNION WITH CHRIST

When you get born again, you get "in Christ-ed." Your spirit is joined to Christ. One translation of 1 Corinthians 6:17 says, "your spirit is joined to the Master." You share a common life, the same life, the same righteousness, the same triumph, and the same blessing. When God looks at you, He sees you in Him, but your faith will not be effectual until you start to acknowledge, confess, and declare your identity in

Christ. You have to acknowledge it. Confession is one way to acknowledge your identity in Christ.

I encourage you to make a daily confession of who you are in Christ. Actually, the Word says to acknowledge it. So "acknowledge" could mean more than just confession. In other words, you declare it, but to acknowledge it would mean to go ahead and act like it.

That is why people need to run, laugh, dance, shout, and daily rejoice by faith. This demonstrates our victory in Christ. That is an acknowledgement of the triumph of Christ. It is an acknowledgement that the victory of Christ is so big that the devil does not have a chance. This is not even a close call. This is a 24-second knockout. Do not hesitate when the Holy Spirit is moving. What He is trying to get you to do is acknowledge who you are in Christ.

The devil is scared of you when you get in the Spirit. When you are in the flesh, thinking of yourself in the natural, you let the devil keep you in the realm of your soul, your reasoning, and your mind. The devil can whip you all day long.

The moment you step out of the natural and out of circumstances, you step right over into who you are in Christ. Your spirit man begins to respond by taking ascendancy over your flesh, your mind, and the circumstances of your faith. Your inner man will rise up and say, "All right, devil, I have had enough of this." The devil will mess with you all day long until you rise up in the Spirit. I like to say it like this: A fly will not land on a hot stove!

I LIKE THAT "I AM" BUSINESS

When I was a senior in high school, I found 130 "in Christ" scriptures, wrote them down, and began to confess them. I put them on a cassette tape. Every morning when I woke up, I heard myself saying, "I am a new creation in Christ, old things are passed away, everything has become new."

I like that "I am" business. The world is full of people who are "trying to be" and "used to be." Have you ever heard somebody say, "He's a wannabe"? "Therefore if any man be in Christ, he IS...," 2 Corinthians 5:17. This is present tense — right now. I am not trying to be, needing to be, hoping to be, or someday going to be. Right now, I am in Christ. I am in "I AM," and so I am. I am a new creation. I am the righteousness of God. I am triumphant.

It is not something I am trying to get or something I am trying to do. It is something in my genes; it runs in my family - I have been born again, and God's life and nature is in me. I am in union with the Champion. I am in union with the righteousness of God. I am in Christ.

SUBSTITUTION AND IDENTIFICATION

When we talk about identification with Christ, it is rather difficult to understand. You say, "Identification with Christ — what does that mean?" That is the center of the Church. It is really the center of all theology.

We are instructed to practice two ordinances in the Church today. One of them is water baptism and the other one is the Lord's Supper. Water baptism is a picture of your identification with Christ in His death, burial, and resurrection (Romans 6:3-6).

The Lord's Supper is to be practiced regularly. Jesus said, "...this do in remembrance of me...this do ye, as oft as ye drink it, in remembrance of me" (1 Corinthians 11:24,25). Eating His flesh and partaking of His blood in the Lord's Supper reveals that you are in union with Him. These are types of your union and your identification with Christ. You are in Him. You are crucified with Him. You are buried with Him, and you are raised up with Him.

BE SWALLOWED UP!

Even the mystery which hath been hid from ages and from generations, but now is made manifest to his saints: To whom God would make known what is the riches of the glory of this mystery among the Gentiles; which is Christ in you, the hope of glory.
- Colossians 1:26,27

Paul shared his revelation in Colossians 1:26,27: "This mystery was hidden for ages and generations, but I am going to to tell you what the secret is. It is Christ in you, the hope of glory." I am swallowed up "in Christ." In other words, man's condition was so bad, he could not be fixed, so God had to kill him and make a new one. Your identification with Christ in His death, burial, and resurrection shows your condition. In Him you died, you were buried, and you were raised from the dead.

IN CHRIST SURGERY

Earlier I told you the story of the California fireman. His hand was burned so badly, the doctors thought they would have to amputate. They decided to try another procedure because of the human body's regenerative powers. They operated on the fireman, inserted his burned hand inside his body, and left it in there. When they removed the hand after a number of days, the skin had begun to grow back again.

God said, "Man's condition is so bad, it looks like he is going to have to be amputated. Before we do that procedure, I can cut Myself open and I will put him inside of Me." On the cross an incision was made, and God put you in Christ.

You were on your way to death, destruction, poverty, and lack, and God said, "There is nothing we can do. We will have to cut ourselves open and put man in us." Paul called this a mystery, but this is redemption — you are in Him. You are joined to Him, identified with Him, and in Him we live and move and have our being (Acts 17:28).

The surgery God performed in the death, burial, and resurrection of Christ was such a massive project, He planned it for thousands of years. Our redemption was such a big project, He had to talk to people for thousands of years just to get someone to believe Him. Because of man's condition, this "in Christ" surgical procedure was the only way man could be saved. The difference between Christianity and all other religions is this one fact: Jesus died, He was buried, and on the third day He arose from the dead.

Mankind did not need a book. We did not need a lesson. We needed a new birth. We needed to be redeemed — we needed the blood of Jesus. We needed His death and His resurrection. You cannot just give people a lesson. That is why every other religion is inferior to Christianity. Jesus died, He was buried, and He arose from the dead. That is the center of the Gospel.

9

THIS CHANGES
EVERYTHING

I remember a time when I became very interested in Albert Einstein and his theory of relativity. I went to the store and bought several books, brought them home and started to read. The problem was, I realized this was way over my head and I actually needed the book, "Albert Einstein For Dummies!" Then I happened across a televised documentary on how Einstein's breakthrough discoveries changed everything for physics.

Einstein's famous theory, $E=MC^2$, was a revolutionary revelation that changed the way scientists thought about how space and time relate to matter and energy. He apologized to Isaac Newton because they ended up having to rewrite all of his physics books! This breakthrough completely changed the way we view the world by opening quantum physics and unlocking the atom and nuclear fission. He said, "This changes everything!"

God, in His great plan of redemption, has done something much greater than Einstein! Let's take a look at His plan of redemption: this changes everything!

THE BLOOD FOREVER CHANGED HEAVEN

Therefore if any man be in Christ, he is a new creature: old things are passed away; behold, all things are become new. - 2 Corinthians 5:17

Weymouth translation says "the old state of things has passed away; a new state of things has come into existence." When Jesus died on the cross, He became sin for us and His death was the death of the sinful old creation.

His blood was the redeeming price paid to buy back humanity from the power of satan. It broke the curse of sin and all its effects. Jesus Christ shed

His blood, defeated sin, was justified in the spirit and then raised from the dead. As our Forerunner, He ascended and took His blood into Heaven itself and placed it there in the heavenly holy of holies. Hebrews 9:12 says, "Neither by the blood of goats and calves, but by his own blood he entered in once into the holy place, having obtained eternal redemption for us."

Jesus' blood opened Heaven for us. "Having therefore, brethren, boldness to enter into the holiest by the blood of Jesus," Hebrews 10:19. Now the blood is on the altar before the Father, forever speaking of mercy and grace. His blood changed everything in Heaven!

THE BLOOD TRIUMPHS OVER HELL

And they overcame him by the blood of the Lamb, and by the word of their testimony; and they loved not their lives unto the death.
- Revelation 12:11

And having spoiled principalities and powers, he made a shew of them openly, triumphing over them in it. - Colossians 2:15

Like the song says, "It reaches to the highest mountain and flows to the lowest valley," Jesus took His blood into hell itself and defeated the lord of death in the confines of human flesh, as a God-Man. He triumphed over Satan himself with His own blood so that we can overcome as a new creation. Jesus' blood overcomes all the power of Satan and hell.

THE BLOOD CHANGES YOUR HEART

And having an high priest over the house of God; Let us draw near with a true heart in full assurance of faith, having our hearts sprinkled from an evil conscience, and our bodies washed with pure water. - Hebrews 10:21, 22

This is the new covenant I will make with my people on that day, says the Lord: I will put my laws in their hearts, and I will write them on their minds. - Hebrews 10:16, NLT

I especially like how the Living Bible puts it in Colossians 1:22, "Christ has brought you into the very presence of God and you are standing there before Him with nothing left against you - nothing that He could even chide you for." Your heart has become the dwelling place for God, the meeting place between a righteous child and a Holy Father God. This changes everything in your heart!

ACCESS GRANTED

We were speaking in a church recently where all the staff wore a card on a string around their necks which had the word "Access" on them. This key card gave them access to different areas and through various doors in the church. I noticed the pastor's card was different. It said, "Unlimited Access." He could go freely into any area in the building others couldn't.

In Christ, by faith in his blood, believers access the most holy place in prayer. One cannot be in God's presence for a moment without being changed! Burdens are lifted, power is increased, revelation granted and the love, joy, faith, and fire of God are experienced. Paul, who knew the formality and deadness of religion and the old law of Moses, wrote about something that happens when any person in Christ accesses the throne room. "In whom we have boldness and access...," Ephesians 3:12.

All of us! Nothing between us and God, our faces shining with the brightness of his face. And so we are transfigured much like the Messiah, our lives gradually becoming brighter and more beautiful as God enters our lives and we become like him. - 2 Corinthians 3:18, Message

And the Lord — who is the Spirit — makes us more and more like him as we are changed into his glorious image. - 2 Corinthians 3:18, NLT

And all of us...are constantly being transfigured into His very own image in ever increasing splendor and from one degree of glory to another; [for this comes] from the Lord [Who is] the Spirit. - 2 Corinthians 3:18, Amplified

Because of the blood of Jesus, any person in Christ has been granted full access to the very presence of God the Father, Son and Holy Spirit. Let us take advantage of all that has been done to open Heaven, overcome hell and open our hearts to the glory of God! May you be granted, by the Spirit's power, a revolutionary revelation! This Changes Everything!

10

THE RIGHTEOUSNESS
OF GOD IN CHRIST

*For he hath made him to be sin for us, who knew
no sin; that we might be made the righteousness
of God in him. - 2 Corinthians 5:21*

*For God took the sinless Christ and poured into
Him our sins. Then, in exchange, He poured
God's goodness into us! - Living Bible*

Here is what happened "in Christ." God made
Jesus to be sin for us. He knew no sin. He took our sin
and our curse and died our death. Jesus was made to
be sin for us so we might be made the righteousness of
God in Him.

What does "righteousness" mean? Righteousness simply means that in Christ your spirit has been made the righteousness of God in Him. Righteousness means that you have right standing with God.

Romans 8:10 says, "And if Christ be in you, the body is dead because of sin; but the Spirit is life because of righteousness." This means that even though you are born again, your body is in a mortal condition because of sin. That is why you have to do something with your body.

Paul said your spirit is alive because of righteousness. When you received Christ, your spirit received eternal life because you were made righteous. You had the very righteousness of God imparted to your spirit.

Paul said that your body is having a problem because of mortality. Your body is dead because of sin. That is why your body still has a bent toward evil. The Bible calls it "the lust of the flesh." Your body still has a certain attraction and desire for evil or sin, but Paul says your spirit is alive because of righteousness.

But if the Spirit of him that raised up Jesus from the dead dwell in you, he that raised up Christ from the dead shall also quicken your mortal bodies by his Spirit that dwelleth in you.
- Romans 8:11

This means you can get so full of the Holy Spirit and the life of God in your spirit, it will neutralize your flesh. That is what you call "putting on" the new man, the new creation. Your spirit will be so full of life, your flesh will be neutralized. You put your flesh in a crucified condition. You crucify the flesh. Your spirit gets caught up with the life of God, and you are happy in Christ. You have been made righteous in Christ.

If you will learn to live and walk in the Spirit, when the devil comes against you, you can say, "All right, I have the blood of Jesus, the name of Jesus, and the Word working in me. I have the anointing of the Holy Spirit now. So, devil, you are underneath my feet. The Greater One lives inside me. I am a new creation in Christ. Old things are passed away. The old person who used to think and act that way is dead and gone. I have been made the righteousness of God in Him."

RIGHTEOUSNESS CONSCIOUSNESS

Putting off the old man and putting on the new man happens by getting your mind renewed with the Word of God. This new man is created in righteousness and through holiness. When you get born again you are not just a forgiven sinner; you have been made the righteousness of God in Christ.

You can be born again and still have a sin-consciousness, constantly having a guilt-consciousness. You can constantly be thinking about the past, your failures, and your weaknesses. You can develop a righteousness-consciousness. When you start acknowledging every good thing that is in you in Christ, however, you develop a consciousness that you have been made righteous. You have been redeemed. You are a new creation. You are triumphant in Christ. As you begin to speak of your redemption, your spirit man will rise up, and bring your body under subjection.

You may ask, "When am I going to be righteous?" All kinds of people have been saved, have been filled with the Holy Spirit, and are praying in other tongues, but they do not know they are righteous yet. They go to church, but they are still trying to be righteous. They think if they can pray long enough, they will be righteous; but they cannot pray long enough to be righteous. They think if they give enough, they will be righteous. They think if they work at the church long enough, they will be righteous; but you cannot work for righteousness.

Titus 3:5 says, "Not by works of righteousness which we have done, but according to his mercy he saved us." Righteousness is imparted to your spirit. Your spirit is recreated in righteousness — it is a gift. You are pleasing to God. You are accepted before God just as if you had never sinned. You are justified or righteous just as if you had never sinned. What if you sin after you get saved?

LIVE BY FAITH

"If we confess our sins, he is faithful and just to forgive us our sins, and to cleanse us from all unrighteousness," 1 John 1:9. If you have been cleansed from all unrighteousness, what does that mean? You have been made righteous again. It has nothing to do with what you feel. You may say, "I still do not feel righteous."

It has nothing to do with your feelings. You are justified by faith in what Christ has done, not by how you feel. Do you feel saved when you get up in the morning? Most people do not get up and say, "I feel saved." Most people do not get up and say, "I feel righteous today. I really feel redeemed. I feel victorious." It has nothing to do with feelings.

The just shall live by faith (Romans 1:17). Righteousness is a part of your faith walk when you acknowledge everything that is in you in Christ. Get up in the morning and say, "I have been made righteous today." When the devil comes against my mind, he brings a picture of failure or weakness. Will the devil bring you a picture? Yes, but you tell him, "That is all right, devil. I know you have a picture, but that does not exist anymore."

YOU ARE RIGHTEOUS NOW

"I, even I, am he that blotteth out thy transgressions for mine own sake, and will not remember thy sins," Isaiah 43:25. God does not remember your sins, but the next verse says, " ...declare thou, that thou mayest be justified."

That means you need to say something with your mouth. Begin to declare, "I have been made righteous by the blood of Jesus. I am the righteousness of God in Christ. I have been forgiven, and I am redeemed by faith. I do not feel like it, I do not look like it, but I declare according to the Word of God that I am righteous. I am a new creation, and this new man has been created in righteousness and true holiness. I am putting him on right now." That is how you put the new man on. It is the gift of God. You are a new creation.

In Smith Wigglesworth's book, *Ever Increasing Faith*, he writes that he went to pray for an Episcopalian priest who wanted to be filled with the Holy Spirit. When he started to pray for him, this priest fell down on his knees. Wigglesworth said the priest prayed the most beautiful prayer that he had ever heard.

When he finished, he began to say, "O God, make me holy. O God, make me holy and clean. O God, sanctify me." When he heard him say that, Wigglesworth said, "Stop, old man! I thought you were saved." The priest said, "I am saved." Wigglesworth answered, "Then you are holy, aren't you? If you have been saved, how could you be a new creature and not be righteous?"

The man said, "Well I am, aren't I? I am righteous. I am holy." He lifted up his hands and got filled with the Holy Spirit right there. This man had been thinking, "If I could just do a little bit more."

In Christ, righteousness has been imparted to your spirit. You are a new creature in Christ. You need to declare that, or the devil will keep you in a sense of guilt and condemnation and cheat you out of God's best blessings for your life. You will never get God's best blessings as long as you live with a sense of condemnation, guilt, and unworthiness. Most people think they really do not deserve anything because of their problems, their weaknesses, or what they did twenty years ago. They have never gotten over it, but the Bible says, "Old things are passed away. Everything has become new."

BEFORE YOU DIE

I heard Jesse Duplantis tell this story about his grandma's birthday. She had been poor all of her life, so they bought her the most beautiful dress they could find. They said, "Granny, won't you wear it to church?" She replied, "I can't wear that dress. It's too pretty. It's just too beautiful. I can't wear it. I'm going to keep it in the closet. I want to be buried in it."

That is exactly the way most Christians are. As soon as you receive Christ, God gives you beautiful new clothes — robes of righteousness. Most Christians look at them and say, "Oh, I couldn't wear that. I am unworthy, so I'll hang it in the closet and wait until I am dead. When I die, I'll be righteous."

You are righteous right now. You are righteous before you die. You are made righteous through faith in Christ. That is how you are made righteous. Throughout the religious world, people struggle with a sense of sin and condemnation.

In Rome, a bronze statue of Peter has the toe worn off by millions of religious people who think they will get blessed if they kiss Peter's toe. In different nations, people crawl for miles on holy days to certain holy places because they think if they can crawl far enough, their sins will be forgiven when they get there.

The good news of the Gospel is that 2,000 years ago on the cross, God was in Christ reconciling and restoring the world to favor with Himself. The Amplified Bible says, "...not counting up and holding against [men] their trespasses, [but cancelling them]..." (2 Corinthians 5:19).

I remember Kenneth E. Hagin telling a story about a vision he had of Jesus. When he saw the glory of Jesus, he fell at Jesus' feet, put his hands on Jesus' feet, and put his face on his hands. He said, "Jesus, I am not worthy to look upon your face." Jesus said,

"Stand up on your feet because I have made you worthy. Stand up on your feet."

Jesus wants you to stand up on your feet and look Him in the eye. Look in the eyes of Jesus. Through His blood, you have been cleansed. You have right standing with God. Your right standing with God is so secure, that He has given you a seat at His own right hand. God Himself can look at you with the most penetrating gaze and cannot find one thing wrong with you. Why? Because you are in Christ. God sees you in Christ.

Philemon 6 says to acknowledge every good thing that is in you in Christ. What are some of the good things? I have been born again. I am a new creation. I have been made righteous now. I am forgiven. I am redeemed.

For your faith to be effective, you must acknowledge those things with the words in your mouth. Then you will win the war against the flesh and the war against your mind. You will win if you will acknowledge every day who you are in Christ.

11

OLD THINGS PASSED AWAY

Crucifixion was a common punishment for criminals in the Roman Empire in New Testament times. Many were put to death in this manner, but we were crucified with only one — the Lord Jesus Christ.

How could you be crucified as a criminal in the Roman Empire? The answer is found in the Apostle Paul's writings to the church in Galatia. Paul said, "I am crucified with Christ: nevertheless I live; yet not I."

We want to get rid of "I" and let Christ live. It is no longer I who lives, but Christ. Remember what I heard T.L. Osborn say: "Little 'I' moved out, and big Christ moved in." It is so hard to get little "I" to move out sometimes because he really likes to run things with his puny little self, but when "big Christ" moves in, just say, "I'm gone. Christ lives in me."

I have been crucified with Christ. Now it is not my old self, but Christ himself who lives in me.
- Galatians 2:20, Noli

I died when Christ died on the cross. I do not live now, but Christ lives in me.
- Cressman

I have been crucified with Christ, and I live now not with my own life but with the life of Christ who lives in me. The life I now live in this body, I live in faith — faith in the Son of God who loved me and sacrificed Himself for my sake. - Jerusalem Bible

I have been crucified with Christ. My own life is dead; it is Christ who lives in me. -Barclay

Yes, I have shared Messiah's crucifixion. I am living indeed, but it is not I that live, it is Messiah whose life is in me.... - Arthur S. Way

Christ took me to the cross with Him, and I died there with Him. - Laubach

I consider myself as having died and now enjoying a second existence, which is simply Jesus using my body. - Distilled Bible

This statement by the Apostle Paul in Galatians 2:20 is the clearest statement about every believer's identification with Christ. Paul, writing under the inspiration of the Holy Spirit says, "We were there in the death, burial, resurrection, triumph, and seating of Jesus Christ." Yet in nearly all of the sermons about what happened on the cross, the listener is identified with someone other than Jesus — the Roman soldiers, Mary, the mother of Jesus, the disciples, or someone in the crowd yelling, "Crucify Him!"

KNOWING THIS

Knowing this, that our old man is crucified with him, that the body of sin might be destroyed, that henceforth we should not serve sin.
- Romans 6:6

Paul wrote the book of Romans to everyone. It was not written just for theologians. Every believer can read the progression of their identification with Christ and who they are in Him. There is a natural progression from Romans 6:6 to Romans 6:11 to Romans 6:14. In Romans 6:6, Paul says, "Knowing this, that our old man is crucified with Him...." When Paul says "old man," who is he talking about? Here is how other translations say it:

Our old sinful nature.... - Romans 6:6, Jordan

The old person I used to be was nailed to the cross with Christ. I have no further role to perform as an offender because I was judged and crucified and the old person is dead and gone. - Cressman

My old inherited self.... - Bruce

Here are a few other things this refers to: My old sick self, my old poor self, my old confused self, my old defeated self, my old condemned self, my old guilty self, and my old sinful self was crucified with Him.

Our former evil IDENTITIES have been executed, so to speak. Our old rebel selves were exterminated and that leaves us no further role to perform as offenders. We were linked with the Divine Representative in death.

- Romans 6:6, Richert

If someone was in the Mafia and decided to testify against the organization, the federal government would have to give him a new identity so he could not be traced. He would have to have a legal identity change including birth certificate, passport, etc.

If anyone from his former lifestyle tried to contact him, his mail, legal notices, and bills would be returned marked, "Return to sender. No such person. No such place." That person no longer exists. That is the power of being dead to sin.

DEAD TO SIN, ALIVE TO GOD

Sin was passed down to you through your genes or your inheritance. The psalmist David said, "Behold, I was shapen in iniquity; and in sin did my mother conceive me" (Psalm 51:5). You do not need to teach children how to sin. They just do it!

That is why all have sinned and come short of the glory of God (Romans 3:23). That is why everyone has to be born again. The only way you can get out of Adam and into Christ is to receive Him. Salvation comes through the death and resurrection of Christ. There is only one escape, and that is an empty tomb! Your old man or your old inherited self was crucified with Christ.

Paul said "knowing this" revealing that this is not all the revelation he wants to share. Let's follow the natural progression in Romans 6 from verse 6 to verse 11. "Likewise reckon ye also yourselves to be dead indeed unto sin, but alive unto God through Jesus Christ our Lord," Romans 6:11.

Sometimes people think if they can just get a certain evangelist to lay hands on them, their problems will go away, but hands can be laid on you and you will still have the same problems. I believe in the laying on of hands and impartation. I believe in the anointing, but Paul is saying, "When you grasp the doctrine of what God has done for you in Christ, it becomes the center of your deliverance, your redemption, and your sanctification." If you try to get it some other way, as soon as the anointing lifts, you have lost it.

The just shall live by faith. Thank God for the anointing, but you must live by faith saying, "I am who God says I am" because the devil is going to come back saying, "Who do you think you are?"

Paul goes from saying "knowing this" in Romans 6:6 to saying "reckon" in Romans 6:11. Reckon or count it to be so by faith. Reckon yourself to be dead indeed unto sin but alive unto God. Sometimes you should say to yourself, "I am dead to sin." One translation says, "...inert and motionless as a corpse in response to sin." When sin comes around, say to it, "I am inert. I am motionless as a corpse. I am dead to sin."

POWER IN THE GOSPEL

The power of the Gospel is seen in both the death and resurrection of Christ. People think only the resurrection is powerful, but the death of Christ is also powerful. In other words, the Gospel gives you the ability not only to speak life, but also to speak death. There is destructive power in the Gospel. The death of Christ puts an end to what you were, and the resurrection of Christ opens up who you are in your new identity.

What do I mean? While I was talking to somebody the other day, he said, "The doctors have told me I have incurable cancer. They have given me a few months to live."

"Hold it just a second — not only do I have a resurrection in the Gospel, but I also have a death. So I curse that cancer, and I command it to die. I speak death to that cancer."

What does that mean? "Death" means "cease to exist." You can speak to things that are ruling in your life and say, "Cease to exist in the name of Jesus! Because of the death and the resurrection of Christ, you die and now life comes in. I have a whole new life." The power of the Gospel is destructive and constructive power. It is destructive to the works of the devil and constructive for the believer.

Paul says, "That I may know him, and the power of his resurrection...being made conformable unto his death" (Philippians 3:10). So we reckon ourselves to be dead indeed unto sin, but we also reckon ourselves to be alive unto God. That means I can hear from Heaven. I can respond to my Father God. "For sin shall not have dominion over you: for ye are not under the law, but under grace," Romans 6:14.

Sin shall not have dominion over you. Old habits, old attitudes, the devil, and the past shall not dominate you. This world shall not dominate you. Shame shall not dominate you. Habits shall not control you. Self-destructive behavior must stop; it shall not have dominion over you. How would you like to hang out with the Apostle Paul for a few weeks? He said, "I died with Christ. I do not live anymore. Christ lives in me." Remember what T.L. Osborn said: "Little 'I' moved out, and big Christ moved in." You could say it this way, "Sick 'I' moved out, and healed Christ moved in. Weak 'I' moved out, and strong Christ moved in. Defeated 'I' moved out, and victorious Christ moved in. Unrighteous 'I' moved out and righteous Christ moved in. Ignorant 'I' moved out, and wise Christ moved in."

The old person I used to be was crucified with Christ. Old things are passed away. God has brought an end to what I used to be and the way I used to be.

NO EVIDENCE OF THE ENEMY

Paul says that God can bring some things to an end, such as certain behavior and influences that have controlled your life. God is able to bring it to an end.

Can you believe God can bring some things to an end?

*But with an overrunning flood he will make
an utter end of the place thereof, and darkness
shall pursue his enemies. What do ye imagine
against the Lord? He will make an utter end:
affliction shall not rise up the second time.*
- *Nahum 1:8,9*

Sin shall not have dominion over you. As soon as the devil chases you, you start chasing the devil. God said, "I will stop this affliction. I will stop this problem. I will stop this condition, and it will never rise again. Not only am I going to stop the enemy, but I am going to destroy the place where the devil got in, so he can never get in there again. I am going to destroy the evidence that he was ever there. You are a brand new creation." People will look at you and ask, "My, what happened to you?"

The body of sin is destroyed. Old things are passed away. God brings your old identity and old influences to an end. He stops them right there. They are all dead, over, and finished.

That is the scripture the Lord gave us about healing for my wife, Trina. The devil came against her with a brain tumor, and the Lord gave us this scripture. He said, "I am going to bring this tumor to an end. I am going to destroy the place it was, so there will be no evidence that it was ever there."

This is true in any area of your life: poverty, defeat, or sickness. In areas of your life where behavior, influences, or things have happened to you that have controlled you, God said, "I am going to bring it to a stop. I am going to bring it to an end. I am going to destroy the evidence it was ever there. You are a brand-new creation. Old things are passed away." There is no inferiority, shame, or poverty on you. There is no evidence on you of what you used to be.

OLD THINGS ARE PASSED AWAY

Lord, You will ordain peace [God's favor and blessings, both temporal and spiritual] for us, for You have also wrought in us and for us all our works. O Lord, our God, other masters besides You have ruled over us, but we will acknowledge and mention Your name only.

They [the former tyrant masters] are dead, they
shall not live and reappear; they are powerless
ghosts, they shall not rise and come back.
Therefore You have visited and made an end of
them and caused every memory of them [every
trace of their supremacy] to perish.
- Isaiah 26:12-14, Amplified Bible

Have you ever had your past come back like a ghost? Verse 14 says, "...[the former tyrant masters] are dead, they shall not live and reappear; they are powerless ghosts...." The devil is the master of deception. You say, "Oh, fear is still there. Confusion is still there. That depression is still there." Even if you recover from a sickness, the devil will try to tell you that the sickness is still there. He will say, "Did you feel that?" You respond, "Oh, I felt that. I felt that."

Isaiah said the tyrants that ruled your past are powerless ghosts. They shall not rise and come back. There is no vacancy in you. God has visited you, made an end of them, and caused every memory of them, and every trace of their supremacy to perish.

Do you know God can bring things to an end, even if they have been there for years? God said,

"Stop! Old things are passed away." You say, "I sure don't feel like it." It has nothing to do with the way you feel. You challenge every attitude, every kind of thought that comes against your mind that contradicts who you are in Christ by saying, "Hold it! You are not staying around here. I am dead to sin, I am alive to God. As a matter of fact, I am God's property, and old things have passed away."

No matter what the devil did, God said, "I swallowed that thing up so there is no trace that it was ever there." When you testify, you will have to tell people that you went through something because they will not be able to tell by looking at you. They will think you have always been blessed, full of joy, prosperous, and triumphant. They will say, "You have never had a problem like I had." And you can say, "Oh, let me tell you where I came from. God brought me out of a horrible pit, out of the miry clay, and He set my feet on a rock" (Psalm 40:2).

SPIRITUAL REALITY

You can never say that God can't identify with your problems. He identifies exactly because Jesus took every condition you can imagine. You might have said, "Lord, You do not understand." He says, "Oh, yes, I have been there and I went there for you so I could bring you out."

I am talking about spiritual reality. Wherever sin and Satan dominated your life, every trace of its supremacy has perished or come to an end. God said, "They will not reappear. They are powerless ghosts. They will never show up again."

The next verse, Isaiah 26:15, says that God brought increase. Sometimes before God can bring increase to you, you have to allow Him through the Word and the Holy Spirit to deal with things that keep coming around in your soul and your life. You have to do that with your identification with Christ.

With the power of the Gospel, you can say, "I was crucified with Christ. I died. Sin shall not have dominion over me. The old person I used to be is dead and gone. The former masters are gone. They have been dethroned. Sin has been dethroned. Satan has been dethroned."

GOD ABOLISHED YOUR ENEMIES ONCE

The book of Hebrews uses the word "once" over and over again. What God did in Christ He did once. You could say it this way: God did it so well, He won't ever have to do it again. Whenever the devil comes around, just say, "It happened once 2,000 years ago. I cannot add anything or take away anything, so I declare that it is mine. I have it now. I am in Christ, so victory is mine."

> *Neither by the blood of goats and calves, but by his own blood he entered in ONCE into the holy place, having obtained eternal redemption for us. - Hebrews 9:12*

Why does it say, "...he entered in once into the holy place...." God did it well enough one time. He does not ever have to do it again. Jesus whipped the devil so badly. He took care of man's condition **once** through the death, burial, and resurrection of Christ.

> *For then must he often have suffered since the foundation of the world: but now once in the end of the world hath he appeared to put away sin by the sacrifice of himself. - Hebrews 9:26*

Other translations say "to do away with," "to abolish," or "to bring it to an end." Through the death of Christ, He brought the dominion, control, and the effect of sin to an end. So Hebrews 9:26 says that through one sacrifice He put an end to sin. He abolished it, put it away, and destroyed it.

Do you believe what God did in Christ is big enough to take care of anything that is messing with you? It does not matter if it is the devil, something from your relatives, something around you, or something messing with your mind and your emotions. What God did in Christ is big enough to take care of it. The Gospel is the power of God. The death of Christ stops sin, and the resurrection of Christ opens up a whole new life.

HE DEALT WITH THE ROOT

God said, "Not only am I going to deal with your sin, your condition, and your problems, I am going to deal with every trace of the memory of it." This is the root of many people's problems. If you have been born again, you are a new creature in Christ. If you allow the memory of your past to continue, it is just as bad as if those things were still there. If you keep thinking about it, the impact is just as if it had happened again.

God told Moses and the children of Israel in

Exodus 14:13, "...Fear ye not, stand still, and see the salvation of the Lord, which he will shew to you today: for the Egyptians whom ye have seen today, ye shall see them again no more for ever." That was hard for them to believe because it was a radical change. They had been under bondage 400 years, but God said, "Today I will stop it, and you will never see your enemies again."

In other words, what had been messing with the children of Israel from generation to generation for the last 400 years and the bondage they had suffered was stopping this day. They would never see these enemies again. The curse stopped and could not go any further. God did not just deal with the fruit; He dealt with the root of their bondage.

When Pharaoh tried to follow the children of God, the ocean just swallowed him up. When the devil tries to follow you around, just hold up the rod of redemption. Declare who you are in Christ and all of a sudden, the death and resurrection of Christ will become a reality and swallow up everything that has tried to hold you in bondage.

The power of the Gospel will cause the enemies that have hounded you and dominated you for years to never dominate your life again. God is saying to you right now, "Apply the Gospel to that, and I will bring an end to that thing. I will stop it so you will never see it again."

God said, "I am going to destroy your past. There will be no trace of it, and it will never reappear. Even the thought of it will disappear. Remember not the former things because I am doing a brand-new thing. Forget the past. Everything has become new. Forget it!"

In Exodus 17:14 God said, "...for I will utterly put out the remembrance of Amalek from under Heaven." God is going to take care of this situation so well, you will not even remember it. The old person you used to be is dead and gone. You might as well forget the past.

Old things have been dealt with through the power of the Gospel and the death and the resurrection of Christ. He hath done it. You were crucified with Him. You died with Him. You were buried with Him. You were raised up together with Him. You have a brand-new identity. You have an identical condition.

You are a brand-new creation. You are seated with Him right now. That is a place of authority. You cannot get any higher than that! You can live and pray from this new place of your identification with Christ.

LIVING IN YOUR IDENTIFICATION
WITH CHRIST

People often say, "Well, that is not my problem, Pastor. But could you tell me how I could get a new refrigerator? My problem is right here." God will give you answers in every area of your life, but you have to get to the root of your blessing, which is right there in who you are in Christ. Once you work out from there, you can get anywhere you want. Anything you need help for — your marriage, prosperity, or healing — is in your identification with Christ.

It is like the Arc of Triumph in Paris, France. The streets of Paris go out like spokes on a wheel from the Arc of Triumph, which is the center of the city. You can get anywhere downtown Paris from the Arc of Triumph. The same is true about Christianity. The center of the Gospel is the death, burial, and resurrection of Christ. You can get anywhere you need to go from there when you see your identification with Christ.

12

MADE ALIVE
WITH CHRIST

In the following passage, Paul says, "I am praying that God will give you a spirit of wisdom and revelation. I am praying that you see what God did for you in Christ, who you are in Christ, and what you have in Him."

> *Cease not to give thanks for you, making mention of you in my prayers; That the God of our Lord Jesus Christ, the Father of glory, may give unto you the spirit of wisdom and revelation in the knowledge of him: The eyes of your understanding being enlightened; that ye*

may know what is the hope of his calling, and
what the riches of the glory of his inheritance in
the saints, And what is the exceeding greatness
of his power to usward who believe, according
to the working of his mighty power, Which he
wrought in Christ, when he raised him from the
dead, and set him at his own right hand in the
heavenly places, Far above all principality, and
power, and might, and dominion, and every
name that is named, not only in this world,
but also in that which is to come: And hath put
all things under his feet, and gave him to be the
head over all things to the church, Which is his
body, the fulness of him that filleth all in all.
- Ephesians 1:16-23

Actually, the Apostle Paul is praying for the Church.
Then he tells three things he wants you to know:

1. What is the hope of His calling
2. What are the riches of the glory of His
inheritance in the saints or believers

3. What is the exceeding greatness of His power toward us who believe according to the working of His mighty power which He wrought in Christ.

WHAT GOD WROUGHT IN CHRIST

"Which he wrought" (Ephesians 1:20) means what He worked, what happened, or what God did in Christ when He raised Him from the dead. What really happened 2,000 years ago in the death, burial, and resurrection of Christ? What was God working out when He raised Christ from the dead? What was wrought or worked in Christ? God "...hath put all things under his feet."

> *Which he wrought in Christ, when he raised him from the dead, and set him at his own right hand in the heavenly places, Far above all principality, and power, and might, and dominion, and every name that is named, not only in this world, but also in that which is to come: And hath put all things under his feet....*
> *- Ephesians 1:20-22*

THE "AND YOU" GOSPEL

In the original Greek, there are no chapter divisions in Paul's letters. The King James Version translators made chapter divisions for ease in writing and reading the Bible. There is really no stopping place in Paul's letters. Actually, he says, "Which is his body, the fulness of him that filleth all in all. And you..." (Ephesians 1:23; 2:1).

You need to underline "and you." What God wrought in Christ, what He did in Christ, was for you. Are you finding yourself in Christ? What God did in Christ and you! I like to call this the "And You" Gospel.

Most churches will talk to you about Jesus. He died, He was buried, He arose from the dead, He is triumphant, He is raised, He is seated, and all power in Heaven and in earth is given to Him. Churches will tell you all about Jesus, but they will make you think Jesus is way up there. He has all power, He has victory, He is blessed, and He is seated. Many churches leave you down here, and tell you you are just a little worm struggling to get along.

Paul lifts Christ to the highest pinnacle in the universe and then says, "And you hath he quickened..."

(Ephesians 2:1). Everything God did in Christ, He did for you, and it is credited to your account as if you did it. You did not actually do it. Jesus did it in your behalf. God did in Christ what He wanted to do in every man, every woman, and every person. He did it in Christ.

Let's see what Paul is saying here. He lifts up Christ and you with Him. Then Paul says, "Christ is the head; we are His body." He is seated far above all principalities, and everything is underneath His feet. He is the head, and we are His body. Are your feet in your head or are they in your body? We are His body, and He is the head. Everything is underneath His feet. If you are the little toe on the body of Christ, you are still seated with Christ far above every principality and every power.

JESUS IS THE HEAD:
WE ARE THE BODY

And hath put all things under his feet, and gave him to be the head over all things to the church, Which is his body, the fulness of him that filleth all in all. -Ephesians 1:22,23

Remember that Christ is the head, and we are His body. Your head and your body go together, right? Jesus is not decapitated! His head and His body go together, too. If He is seated, you are seated, and if He is blessed, you are blessed.

Your head and your body go by the same name. You do not have one name for your head and a different name for your body. When you go into a bank, you do not open up different accounts for your head and your body. No, you are one.

1 Corinthians 6:17 says, "...he that is joined unto the Lord is one spirit." Your identification with Christ is your identity in Him. You are one with Him. You are joined to Him. Whatever is in Him, as the head, is also in the body. Whatever belongs to the head belongs to the body.

Jesus gives us another analogy in John 15:5: "I am the vine, ye are the branches...." The same things that are in the vine flow in the branches. Your identity is wrapped up with who you are in Christ and what you have in Him. You are one with Christ, joined to Him.

Ephesians 2:1 says, "And you hath he quickened...." Whatever God did in Christ, you can say, "And in me, too. I was there. He took me with Him. I was crucified with Him. I died with Him. I was buried with Him. I

188

was made righteous with Him. I was raised with Him, and I am seated with Him." Whatever God did in Christ, He really did in you because you are in Him.

HE GAVE US THE SAME LIFE

And you hath he quickened, who were dead in trespasses and sins; Wherein in time past ye walked according to the course of this world, according to the prince of the power of the air, the spirit that now worketh in the children of disobedience: Among whom also we all had our conversation in times past in the lusts of the flesh, fulfilling the desires of the flesh and of the mind; and were by nature the children of wrath, even as others. But God, who is rich in mercy, for his great love wherewith he loved us, Even when we were dead in sins, hath quickened us together with Christ, (by grace ye are saved;) And hath raised us up together, and made us sit together in heavenly places in Christ Jesus.
- Ephesians 2:1-6

This is where we get our identification with Christ. God has *quickened* us with Christ. What does the word *quickened* mean? The word quicken means He made us alive together with Christ.

Let's look at the tenses of the verbs in this scripture. "And you hath he quickened...," Ephesians 2:1. The Gospel is not the good news that God wants to help you. The Gospel is the good news that God has already helped you. God has already done something for you. It has already been accomplished, and it already belongs to you. It is yours right now.

> *...because of and in order to satisfy the great and wonderful and intense love with which He loved us, Even when we were dead [slain] by [our own] shortcomings and trespasses, He made us alive together in fellowship and in union with Christ — He gave us the very life of Christ Himself, the same new life with which He quickened Him....*
> *- Ephesians 2:4,5, Amplified*

God gave us the very life of Christ Himself; the same new life with which He quickened Him. This is our identification with Christ. The identical life that raised Christ from the dead is in you. You are identified with Christ because you share a common,

identical life. Whatever that life did in Christ, it does
in you. The same life that is in Christ is also in you.

> *But if the Spirit of him that raised up Jesus*
> *from the dead dwell in you, he that raised up*
> *Christ from the dead shall also quicken your*
> *mortal bodies by his Spirit that dwelleth in you.*
> *- Romans 8:11*

God did not give Christ one kind of life when
He was raised from the dead and then say, "We will
need to filter this down to give it to people because
we do not want to give them the same quality. We
will need to give them something different." Instead,
God said, "I am going to give man the same life I
gave to Christ when I raised Him from the dead; the
same life that is in Me; the same life that quickened
Christ." It is the same life that is in you. If it is the
same life, we have an identical life. We have a match.
Paul says in 2 Corinthians 4:13, "We having the same
spirit of faith...." That means identically the same
spirit of faith, the same life, the same Holy Spirit, and
the same power that quickened Christ also quickens
us. The devil is afraid of you whenever you find out
that you have the same things in you that Jesus had

in Him and has in Him right now. So Paul says, "The same life, the same spirit, and the same power that quickened Christ dwells in you, right now— identically the same stuff." You really could not be defeated in life if you have what Paul says and what he is praying for you to get.

UNFOLDING THE WAY GOD SEES

He says, "I am praying that you see what God did for you in Christ, your identification with Christ, who you are in Christ, and what you have in Him." He said, "I am praying that God will give you a spirit of wisdom and revelation." What is revelation? It is an unfolding and opening up.

Revelation knowlege is different than sense knowledge. Revelation knowledge unfolds you to the way God sees you and what God says about you. Revelation knowledge is not what your parents said about you, what you have said about yourself, what other people have said about you, or even what your own natural experience says abotu you. Revelation knowledge simply says, "I am who God says I am. I have what God says I have. I can do what God says I can do." That's the bottom line of revelation knowledge.

This is the first of the Law of Identification with Christ (Chapter 4). Once you understand your identification with Christ, you can no longer identify with who you used to be. You can no longer identify with failure. You can no longer identify with sin-consciousness. You can no longer identify with poverty by saying, "I am just so poor." You can not identify with that anymore! You are identified with Christ.

Many churches and ministries have great passion plays. They try to make them as realistic as possible with a cross, angels flying on cables through the air, people dressed in biblical costumes, donkeys, camels, and sheep. They do their best to make you see the crucifixion and the resurrection of Christ. There is nothing wrong with that. I enjoy passion plays because they illustrate the power of the death and resurrection of Christ. You can go to a passion play to see the death and resurrection of Christ and cry, but unless you understand your identification with Christ, you will walk out of there with the same behavior you had before you were moved with emotion for an hour. You have tried to emotionally attach yourself to the death and resurrection of Christ, but you are not attached emotionally; you are attached spiritually by revelation knowledge. The Holy Spirit shows you what happened and your place in the death and resurrection of Christ.

"Knowing that God will give you a spirit of wisdom and revelation." What is revelation? It is an unfolding and opening up. Revelation knowledge is different than sense knowledge. Revelation knowledge unfolds to you the way God sees you and what God says about you. Revelation knowledge is not what your parents said about you, what you have said about yourself, what other people have said about you, or even what your own natural experience says about you. Revelation knowledge simply says, "I am who God says I am. I have what God says I have. I can do what God says I can do." That's the bottom line of revelation knowledge.

This is the first of The Laws of Identification With Christ (Chapter 4). Once you understand your identification with Christ, you can no longer identify with who you used to be. You can no longer identify with failure. You can no longer identify with sin-consciousness. You can no longer identify with poverty by saying, "I am just so poor."

The Holy Spirit shows you what happened and

your place in the death and resurrection of Christ. You can have a sentimental view of the cross. You can have crosses on your wall and Bibles all over your house and still never really know your identification with Christ. But once you have "the spirit of wisdom and revelation...and the eyes of your understanding being enlightened that you may know..." (Ephesians 1:17,18), you will understand.

The Greek word for "understanding" is also the word for "heart." The eyes of your heart are flooded with the light of the glorious Gospel. You see what God did in the death, burial, and resurrection of Christ. You see that everything God did was for you. You can say what Paul said in Galatians 2:20: "I am crucified with Christ: nevertheless I live; yet not I, but Christ liveth in me...."

DIFFERENT VIEWPOINTS

The death, burial, and resurrection of Christ can be studied from a number of different viewpoints. Many times people study them from a certain viewpoint. They see Jesus on the cross, but they identify with one of the thieves or the Roman soldiers, who were saying, "Crucify Him!" They even identify with some of the disciples who ran off or with the crowd. What God saw in the death, burial, and resurrection of Christ is that you were identified with Christ Himself.

What happened to Christ happened in your behalf, so you were crucified with Him. You died with Him. You descended into the grave with Him, but on the third day you were declared righteous with Him. You were made alive with Him. You triumphed with Him. You were raised with Him. You sat down with Him. You reign with Him. He is the Head and you are a member of His body. Whatever is in Him is in you.

Paul says you get "in" at the cross, or the death of Christ. The Laubauch's translations of Galatians 2:20 state it this way: "Christ took me to the cross with Him, and I died there with Him. Now it is not my old self but Christ Himself who lives in me." He lives in me. He lives in you.

THE SAME STUFF

Paul's understanding is that Christ lives in you and me. The Distilled Bible says, "I consider myself as having died and now enjoying a second existence, which is simply Jesus using my body" (Galatians 2:20).

What does this mean? It means you have the same righteousness, the same life, the same power, the same triumph, the same spirit, the same stuff, and the same blessing Christ has, and you are an identical heir of God and joint-heir with Christ. You are in Him, and He is in you. You are joined to Him. Your spirit is joined to Christ. This makes it difficult to be defeated, doesn't it?

On the cross, Jesus was made to be sin for us. He took our sin. He died our death, or He took our place. When you see the cross, you see man's condition in Adam, or man's condition outside of God. Man is a sinner separated from God. Man is cursed, and you see the way man really is. Jesus died the death of the sinner, so He was treated the same as a sinner would be in the sight of God.

He took the same condition you had, so when He was raised from the dead, you could have the same life, the same righteousness, and the same power. You have an identical condition. He took your place in His death. You take the same life He has in His resurrection.

13

SEATED WITH CHRIST

He gave us life together with Christ. And hath
raised us up together and made us sit together in
heavenly places in Christ Jesus.
- Ephesians 2:5,6, Phillips

Before you can stand against the wiles of the devil,
and before you can walk the Christian walk, you must
learn how to sit. I once read a book by Watchman Nee
called, *Sit, Walk, and Stand.* It is a short but powerful
book about the book of Ephesians. There is a very
simple progression here: sit, walk, and stand. People
want to stand against the devil as in Ephesians 6, or

they want to learn how to walk the Christian walk in Ephesians 4, but they have never learned how to sit from Ephesians 2. You must take your place in the finished work of Christ. By "finished," I mean Jesus has already done everything He is going to do about the devil, your righteousness, and your victory in life. He has already (past tense) done it, or taken care of it.

He has defeated the devil, spoiled him, stripped him, disarmed him, established your righteousness, given you the victory, sat down, and said, "It is all over,. I am seated for above everything, and I did it for you." That is the why the Gospel is not "God can." pr "God wants to." No, God has already taken care of the devil, your righteousness, and your victory in life. You don't have to do it. All you have to do is sit down!

THE FINISHED WORK OF REDEMPTION

Take your place, first of all in Christ, in the finished work of redemption, and sit down. You give the devil the most trouble when you sit down! Often people are fighting themselves and may other things. If you are fighting everything in the natural, you are going to lose. "Not by might, nor by power, but by my spirit..." Zechariah 4:6. So take your place in Christ, and sit down.

Satan is far below you, and you are far above him. Christ is the head, and you are in His body. You have the same account, the same righteousness, the same life, the same victory, and the same authority Christ has. Just sit down and say, "Ha, ha, ha, devil, you cannot do this to me. I am seated with Christ." You had better get your binoculars out to see him because he is so far below you. He is far below your feet even if you are the little toe in the body of Christ.

> *And hath raised us up together, and made us*
> *sit together in heavenly places in Christ Jesus,*
> *- Ephesians 2:6*

God is not going to do it. You do not have to talk Him into doing it because He has already done it. He hath raised us up together.

You can deal with life from a different perspective now. You can deal with your problems from a position of triumph and victory, not from a place of trying to get the victory. You can say, "I am taking my place. I am going to sit down right now, and I am going to rest in what Jesus has already done. I do not need to fight in this battle. God fights in the battle and gives me the victory."

We, ourselves, now exercise an authority like that which Christ has in he presence of God.
- Ephesians 2:6, Johnson

God raised us from the dead with Christ, and gave us a place to sit with Him in heaven.
- Cressman

Together with Christ Jesus and in Him, He raised us up with Him to rule with Him in the heavenly world. - Kleist and Lily

Being seated at the right hand of God is a picture of your authority as a believer. You are not helpless, hopeless, or trying to make something work. No, you already have an established authority seated with Christ at the right hand of God. He raised us up and made us sit down together with Him in the heavenly world.

A PLACE OF AUTHORITY

We live so much in the natural that our whole life is spent taking care of natural things with our reasoning. When you get in the Spirit, you learn to take your place by faith and the Spirit. You can sit down and say, "Devil, you have no power over me. You have no dominion over me. I have been delievered from the power of darkness. I have been translated into the kingdom of the Son of God. I am seated with Christ and now I have authority."

From this place of authority at the right hand of God, you can make some announcements. It is a place of supernatural advantage and access. You can say, "Father God, now I have access into your presence. I am going to pray from this place. I am going to live from this place. I am going to speak the word of faith from this place where I am seated in Christ."

Do not pray from down here by saying, "O, Lord, I am down here on earth. I am having such a hard time, and the devil is everywhere down here." Instead, pray from your place in Christ where triumph is already yours. By faith, climb up in the Spirit to who you are in Christ, take the Word of God, and say, "O, Father God, it is so good to be seated at your right hand, to call you Daddy, and to be an heir of God and a joint-heir with Jesus Christ. Oh, Father, it is so good to fellowship with You and enjoy the benefits of Heaven. I do not have to wait until I get to Heaven to be blessed. I am already seated in heavenly places. I have the same life, the same joy, the same peace, the same victory, and the same blessing."

The Cornish translation reads this way: "God raised us out of it all with Christ, and sat us down on the right hand of power with Him and gave us dominion" (Ephesians 2:6). He gave us dominion. Jesus got back the dominion that Adam lost, and you are in Him.

The Carpenter's paraphrase of Ephesians 2:6 reads like this: "We found ourselves not only risen from death but in Christ who is in Heaven, and therefore in the Heavenly realm ourselves." That is my favorite one. We found ourselves not only risen from death, but in Christ who is in Heaven. Therefore, we are in the heavenly realm ourselves.

LIVING IN THE HEAVENLY REALM

What is it like to be in the heavenly realm? What is it like to go beyond the veil of this earth, enter into the Holy of Holies by the blood of Jesus, and live in the heavenly realm? You not only have fellowship with the Father, but you have authority in this world.

When you pray and when you speak, things change in your family, your business, your body, and in nations. You speak and pray from this place of authority seated at the right hand of God. God is not going to do this for you; He has already done His part.

You say, "I can't figure this all out with my head." That is why Paul said, "I am praying that God will give you a spirit of wisdom and revelation so the eyes of your heart will be flooded with light." The Holy Spirit will give you a flash of revelation and you can say, "Glory to God, I believe I am going to laugh a while." You are not down here struggling. You are up there in heavenly places saying, "Ha, ha, ha. Victory is mine!"

Does that mean you do not have any trials? No, you have trials and adversity, but you face everything from your position in Christ. He hath quickened us together with Christ. He hath raised us up together and made us sit down together with Christ. Relax and sit down.

Once you take your seat, you can walk, and then you will be able to stand. If you are having a hard time standing against the devil when he comes against you, you need to take your seat. You need to see your identification with Christ in His death, His burial, and His resurrection.

BE A "YES" MAN

All the promises of God in Him are "yes." I have a pastor friend in Chicago who has a toy "yes man" sitting on his desk. He is dressed nicely in a little suit, his hair is perfect, and his smile is just right. The little "yes man" has a switch on his back and is voice-activated. Anytime my friend is having a conflict and cannot find anybody to agree with him, his "yes man" agrees with him.

My friend tells this "yes man" what he is thinking and asks, "What do you think?" The "yes man" then responds, "I couldn't agree more," or "Wow! You're a genius!"

God is a genius, and I am the "yes man." Whenever I am reading the Word, God says, "You are a new creature in Christ." I say, "I couldn't agree more. Wow, you are a genius!" You don't have to be smart to be a "yes man." All you have to do is agree. You do not have to thing anything up. All you have to do is just agree with what God said.

For all the promised of God in him are yea, and
in him Amen, unto the glory of God by us.
- 2 Corinthians 1:20

Too often, you put too much pressure on yourself, but you do not have to come up with the victory or the answer. All you need to do is open your Bible and say, "Oh, I have the Word right here. I have the Good News already. God says, 'I AM that I AM.' I couldn't agree more!"

We do not have to come up with answers. All we have to do is take the Word, find the "in Christ" scriptures, and be a "yes" person. In Christ all the promises of God are "yes." How do you become a "yes" person? You agree with God. You say, "I am who God says I am. I have what God says I have. I can do what God says I can do." Say the same thing God says about you: I am in Him. He is in me. I do not have to work this thing out because I am in Him. I was with Him; therefore, I am in Him, and I am seated with Him right now.

Now look at that again: "...all the promises of God in him are yea...." In other words, God is not saying, "Yes, no, or maybe." Anything God has ever promised in Christ is "yes." It is affirmative; no question about it. You do not have to wonder if God might or might not want to bless you, help you, or give you what you have asked for. He said, "It is an absolute yes in Him!"

Paul said that for your faith to become effective, you need to acknowledge those things (Philemon 6). You need to do that morning, noon, and night. You need to spend time writing down scriptures that use the two words "In Christ" or "In Him." Then begin to declare, "That is who I am, and that is what I have. I am in Him. Right there is where I am. I am in Him."

> *For as many as were the promises of God in Christ is the yes that fulfills them; therefore through Christ again let the Amen rise through us to the glory of God.*
> *- 2 Corinthians 1:20, Twentieth Century*

SO BE IT

Do you know what "Amen" means? It means "so be it." If you are in church and say, "Amen," you are saying, "So be it." You ought to think about what you "Amen." Some people just say "amen" at timed intervals. They are not even paying attention. One man was preaching and said, "You know millions of people are going to hell every day." Then he said, "Amen." That means, "So be it. Let them go to hell, man. I don't care." You need to be careful when you say "amen." You can go to church and walk out in the same condition you came in, even though you said "Amen," "Glory," and "Hallelujah" in all the right places. When you go home, you act the same way you did before you went to church.

Paul is saying, "Amen, so be it." Jesus is the Amen. Jesus, through His death, burial, and resurrection came and said, "So be it" to everything God has ever promised. He fulfilled it and brought the reality of it into the economy of God. It is no longer just a promise or just some theology; it is an absolute reality.

REDEMPTION REALITY

When we talk about your redemption and who you are in Christ, we are not talking about some figment of your imagination or some religious thing. We are talking about an absolute reality of redemption and righteousness. We are talking about living in the reality that you are redeemed, righteous, victorious, and blessed. You are living in the reality that old things are passed away, everything has become new, and now you are a new creation.

Jesus is the "Amen." He brought the reality of redemption into the realm of human experience and into your life. The Twentieth Century New Testament says, "...so let the Amen rise through us to the glory of God." You need to respond to Him by saying, "Amen, so be it."

If God said, "It is yes, affirmative, it is yours," you can say, "So be it. It is so. It is mine, and I have it now. I am not trying to get it. I do not hope to get it. I am in Christ, and I boldly declare and acknowledge right now the good things that are in me in Christ. Yes, affirmative, so be it. It is so; it is not trying to be so, ought to be so, or need to be so. It just is so right now. It is mine. I have it now."

The Wood translation says, "Therefore our human part is but to say Amen to God through Him" (2 Corinthians 1:20). Paul says, "It is up to you to say 'Amen.'" Really, the main reason you say "amen" is to say, "So be it, it is so, it is a fact, it is true in my life, and I boldly acknowledge today that I am who God says I am."

GRACE VS. LEGALISM

A.J. Gordon in his book, "In Christ," says:

Through these two words "in Christ" we get a profound insight into the divine method of salvation. God does not work upon the soul by itself; bringing to bear upon it, while yet in its alienation and isolation from Him, such discipline as shall gradually render it fit to be reunited to Him. He begins rather by reuniting it to Himself, that through this union He may communicate to it that divine life and energy, without which all discipline were utterly futile. The method of grace is precisely the reverse of the method of legalism. The latter is holiness in order to union with God; the former, union with God in order to holiness.

The author says that God's method of salvation is that He does not work on you while you are isolated from Him to gradually render you fit to be reunited to Him. Legalism has God operating on you apart from Himself, but grace begins by uniting you to God, and through that union supplying the life and power necessary to bring you into His holiness.

Grace is the opposite of legalism. Legalism says that you are not good enough yet. Grace says because of what Christ has done, instantly your spirit is joined to Christ. Through that union, God supplies what you need to change you. Everybody else is trying to change apart from who they are in Christ.

Legalism is so sad because by the time you do everything they want you to do (change your hair, your clothes, and do everything their way), you still haven't done enough. You will still have to live in sin-consciousness for the rest of your life because you have never done quite enough to be right with God.

Grace is just the opposite. God welcomes you because of faith in Christ. He takes you right in and gives you His righteousness. Nothing is more striking than the breadth of application which this principle of union with Christ has in the Gospel. Gordon said that the applications of this are endless. Gordon continues:

> *Thus, Christ in taking man up into Himself, takes all that belongs to Him. Instead of rending him away from all of his natural connections, he embraces all these with him in Himself that*

he may sanctify them all. And not only is this true but the opposite and far more wondrous fact, namely, that Christ, in raising man into union with Himself, raises Him into all that belongs to Him, into His divine life, and to partnership with His divine work. When God raised you together with Christ, He raised you up into everything that belongs to Him, His life, and partnership with His work. You die in His death, rise in His resurrection, ascend in His ascension, and are seated with Him at the Father's right hand. When you start talking in tongues, you just went into a heavenly session with Jesus to take care of business. So marked is this latter fact, that has led some to speak of the events of the Christian life as affording "a striking parallel to those of Christ's.

The events of the Christian life are so striking in Paul's letter, they cause some theologians to say there is a parallel between the events of Christ and the events of the Christian life. For example, Jesus was crucified, and the believer was crucified. Jesus died, and the believer died. Jesus was buried, and the believer was buried. Jesus was raised, and the believer was raised.

Gordon says:

> *But there is no parallel. Parallels never meet, while the very glory and the mystery of the The Power of Identification With Christ believer's life is that it is one with the Savior's and inseparable from it. It is not a life running along side of his, and taking shape and direction from it. It is His life re-enacted in his followers; the reproduction in them of those events which are immortal in energy and limitless in application.*

Your life is not a life that runs parallel to Christ like you were trying to be like Christ. The mystery and the glory of the believer's life is that your life is one with Him; you are joined to Him. His life is in you. In application, you died to sin, but now you are alive unto God. The death and the resurrection of Christ are reproduced — limitless in application and immortal in energy. That means there is power in the Gospel.

JESUS PEOPLE

Your identification with Christ causes you to establish a whole new identity in Him. In the late

1960's and 1970's, youth revivals attracted thousands of teenagers. Kids came in bell-bottom blue jeans and strange hairdos, and loud Christian rock 'n' roll music blasted forth. Regular church people could not stand it. They called them Jesus People.

Out of this Jesus Movement came some of the greatest pastors, evangelists, and missionaries today. They fell in love with Jesus. They did not love all the sentimental extras that came with religion. They just loved Jesus. They jumped in there and some great revivals resulted!

Isaiah 59:19 says, "...When the enemy shall come in like a flood, the Spirit of the Lord shall lift up a standard against him." This whole generation was going down the tubes, but the Holy Spirit lifted up a standard. He raised up some people who were not like church people, and they turned the tide. Instead of losing a whole generation to rock music, there was a great revival.

IDENTIFIED WITH JESUS

You ask, "I know I have been born again, but what do I need to do?" Sit down first, and take your place in Christ and in the finished work of Christ.

You can learn how to walk by taking one step at a time, by acknowledging who you are in Him. Next, you will learn how to stand when the devil comes against you and challenges you by saying, "That is not so in your life."

You can answer, "Oh, yes, it is so. I am righteous. I am a new creature. I am redeemed. Oh, yes, I am victorious. I am who God says I am. I am blessed. I cannot help but be blessed. It runs in my family. My Father God has it, my older brother Jesus has it, and the same blessing that is in them runs in my family. I am the head and not the tail. I am above and not beneath." It may take a while before your circumstances change, but they will have to change.

The
Pursuit of
Identification

14

A HAPPY MAN IN CHRIST

The Apostle Paul is the original "in Christ" preacher and teacher. Paul was a new creature preacher. He was a new creature — a new man. He was Saul when he met Jesus. Somebody said his experience with Jesus was so strong, it knocked the "S" off the front of his name and put a "P" there.

In other words, he is a Paul instead of a Saul. God is in the people-making business. No one else has been able to make a person. God is the original manufacturer. If there is something wrong with you, He can make you over again. Whether it is your spirit, your soul, or your body, He has the materials necessary to correct your problem.

"IN HIM-ERS"

I have been preaching this since I was seventeen years old. People start to call you different names if you preach on something a lot. If you preach on faith, they say, "He is one of those 'faith' people." If you preach prosperity, they say, "He is one of those 'prosperity' people." If you preach healing, they say, "He is one of those 'healing' people."

When I was a youth pastor in North Louisiana in 1975 and 1976, I had a Christian radio program called "Rock 'n' Roll Preacher." I taught on who you are in Christ on a secular station.

I preached on "in Christ" a lot, so they said, "He is one of those *in Him-ers*. That means you have put a lot of emphasis on who you are in Him and not on who you are in yourself. The emphasis is not on who you are because of your denominational affiliation, but on who you are because of your relationship to the Lord Jesus Christ. I am a new creature preacher!

EXPERIENCE JESUS

"For whether we be beside ourselves, it is to God: or whether we be sober, it is for your cause," 2 Corinthians 5:13. In other translations Paul simply said, "If we have lost our minds, it is God's fault."

Many people thought Paul was crazy because he had such a radical experience with Jesus Christ. His life turned in a totally different direction. I am sure his mama, his daddy, his kinfolks, and his old friends thought he was crazy and had lost his mind.

I believe your experience with Jesus ought to be so strong and put such a dividing line in your life, that your old friends do not even want to be around you anymore! They will say, "We do not want to be around him. He is always talking about Jesus, reading the Bible, praising God, and wanting to go to church."

Paul was not a gang member or a drug addict, but Paul was hooked on religion. He was bound by religion and good works. When he met Jesus, Paul found that knowing Jesus was greater than any effort, religion, tradition, or anything else that man could attempt.

Religion and tradition bring death; however Jesus brings life and a living experience with Him. Jesus is not a bunch of rules and regulations. Sometimes people get caught up in rules and regulations, but Paul said, "You need to get caught up with who you are in Christ and who you are in Him. You need to experience Jesus!"

Many people, especially the Pharisees, probably thought Paul was crazy. When he was on the road to Damascus, he met Jesus and was never the same. He spent a number of years getting a revelation of "in Christ" and who you are in Christ, so he used this phrase over and over again. Paul said, "If I have lost my mind, it is God's fault, but I am trying to stay sober for your sake."

A man told me one time he was afraid if he thought like me, he would lose his mind. I said, "If you knew how little you have to lose, you would let it go." Some people are holding on to their little minds when they could "lose" their minds and get the mind of Christ.

Have you ever had the Holy Spirit come upon you with just such a revelation of the goodness of God and what God has done for you in Christ? You may feel like you have lost your mind. You may want to shout, jump, run, and roll on the floor! If that has never happened to you, you have never really had a good revelation of what God has done for you in Christ.

Once you see what God has done for you in Christ is so big and so good, you will want to jump, run, laugh, and shout!

So Paul said, "Sometimes I just get beside myself when I start thinking about Jesus — what God has done for me in Jesus, who I am in Jesus, and what I have in Jesus. I am not the same person I used to be. I am a new person in Jesus. Oh, the possibilities that are mine in Jesus! When I start thinking about the access I have to the Father in Jesus and the Holy Spirit living in me because I am in Christ, I feel like I am losing my mind."

You need to have a daily soak or a daily saturation of the reality of who you are and what you have "in Christ." A daily saturation, not just a confession, allows the Holy Spirit to bring those things into your experience until old things are passed away and everything has become new.

KNOW PEOPLE AFTER THE SPIRIT

And that he died for all, that they which live should not henceforth live unto themselves, but unto him which died for them, and rose again.
- 2 Corinthians 5:15

Jesus died in your place and rose again in your place. He died in your behalf and rose again in your behalf. He died on your account and rose again on your account.

> *Wherefore henceforth know we no man after the flesh: yea, though we have known Christ after the flesh, yet now henceforth know we him no more. - 2 Corinthians 5:16*

Paul said we used to know Jesus after the flesh, but we do not know Him that way anymore because He has ascended to Heaven. We now know Him after the Spirit. We do not know Him after the flesh because He is not walking around here in a body anymore.

Some translators reverse this to say that since we know Christ after the Spirit, we do not assess any man after the flesh anymore. In other words, I do not know you naturally. Paul said, "I am going to show you how you can know who people really are — not just who they are naturally by studying their roots, who their parents were, what country they came from, what race they are, or what language they speak. I am going to show you how you can know who people really are in Christ, in the Spirit."

A BRAND-NEW PERSON

"Therefore if any man...." this means this will work for anyone. "Therefore if any man be in Christ...." It does not say if any man be in church. You can be in church and be the same old stinking thing you have always been, but when you get "in Christ," you cannot stay the same. You are changed.

"Therefore if any man be in Christ, he is...." Paul was not talking about males only; he was talking about mankind — man or woman. "Therefore if any man be in Christ, he [or she] is a new creature...." One translation says it this way, "a new species of being that never existed before." When you get born again, you are not just a forgiven sinner. You have been recreated. In the Old Testament, sins were only covered and forgiven. Because of the death and resurrection of Christ, you have not simply been forgiven; you have become a whole new person, a whole new creation. You are not just a forgiven sinner. You are a brand-new person. God has recreated you.

PRESENT TENSE

I like the present tense of 2 Corinthians 5:17. It excites me to see that, "Therefore if any man be in Christ...." When you are born again, you be in Christ. Whatever is true of anyone else who is in Christ is true about you. If you be in Christ, then what be in Christ be in you.

Hebrews 11:1 says, "Now faith is...." This is present tense. In other words, if it is going to be, it is not faith. If it used to be, it is not faith. God introduced Himself to Moses by saying, "I AM that I AM."

Somebody said, "What is God's last name?" AM is God's last name. That is present tense. When you get in Christ, you am in Him. Whatever am in Him am in you right now. Whatever be in Him, be in you. You are not trying to be, not hoping to be, not going to be. Right now you be in Him. Now faith is.

The moment you declare who you are in Him, your faith will work. Otherwise, you will always try to be, hope to be, and want to be. This is the miracle of the new birth. Right now, in Him, you are a new creature. In Him, you have been made righteous. In Him, you are triumphant. In Him, you are redeemed. In Him, you have peace with God.

You need to forget who you are naturally and get up every morning seeing who you are in Him. You are complete in Him. So Paul said, "If any man [person] be in Christ, he is...." I am in Him, and I Am is in me!

BRAGGING ON REDEMPTION

The reason that the majority of Christians are weak, though they are earnest, yet they are weak, is because they have never dared to make a confession of what they are in Christ.
- E.W. Kenyon

People think it makes God happy for them to talk about everything they are not. Would it make you happy if your kids came in every day and told you everything they are not?

Some people get upset with this because they think they are being humble when they continually run themselves down. You are not just being ignorant; you are opening the door to the devil. We know that in ourselves we can do nothing. We have already proven that!

Philemon 6 tells you to acknowledge every good thing that is in you in Christ. You need to acknowledge who you are in Christ and the good things that are in you because you are in Him. In other words, you are not really boasting of who you are in the flesh; you are boasting of what God has accomplished for you in Christ. You are not bragging on yourself; you are bragging on who you are in Him. You are bragging on redemption.

John G. Lake said that in all of your preaching and teaching you must always leave people with the consciousness of the triumph of Christ. Before you leave church, you should be conscious and aware of the triumph of Christ and who you are in Him. There should be a song in your spirit. No matter what the devil is doing, something in you should say, "I feel like singing! I want to shout!"

I THINK MYSELF HAPPY

The Apostle Paul could be shipwrecked, snake bit, beaten in the head, left for dead, or be in the middle of the prison and still say, "I feel like singing right now because the Greater One is in me." How would you like to be chained to Paul for about a year and a half? Paul was not some confused, lonely, bitter preacher.

He stood before King Agrippa after thirty years and said, "Oh, king, I think myself happy" (Acts 26:2).

You can think yourself happy or you can think yourself sad. Paul said, "I am a happy man." He could have said a lot of things. He could have said, "I am a lonely man. You know, never did get married." He could have said, "I feel like a rejected man because I lost a lot of friends." He could have said, "I am a tired man. I have been working at this for thirty years." Standing there in chains before one of the rulers of the Roman Empire, Paul said, "I am a happy man."

King Agrippa, his sister Bernice, Governor Festus, and all the military leaders, lawyers, and other prominent people were there when Paul came in. They wanted to poke fun at him — they wanted to mock him — but you cannot ridicule a happy man. When he entered he said, "I am a happy man." He probably had the least reason to be happy of anybody in that whole crowd. Everybody else had power and money. They also had influence, fame, and prestige, but Paul said, "I am a happy man. I wish all of you were as happy as I am."

They wanted to talk about other issues, but Paul said, "Let me tell you what the main issue is here. Jesus Christ came to this earth; He died on the cross;

He arose from the dead. I met Him personally. He is alive." Before it was over, King Agrippa was shaking because conviction hit that whole place. Paul turned the occasion into an altar call and said, "Does anyone want to come forward and receive Jesus?"

The king said, "Almost thou persuadest me to be a Christian" (Acts 26:28). He will be the most upset man in hell because he had a testimony from the greatest preacher other than the Lord Jesus Christ, and he said, "I don't have time right now. I have my friends here, and this is a little embarrassing. I am almost persuaded. I'll talk to you later." King Agrippa died a poor, broken man. Paul identified himself in 2 Corinthians 12:2 simply as a man in Christ.

> *I knew a man in Christ above fourteen years ago, (whether in the body, I cannot tell; or whether out of the body, I cannot tell; God knoweth;) such an one caught up to the third heaven...and heard unspeakable words, which it is unlawful for a man to utter.*

He said, "I am a happy man." One translation of Acts 26:2 says, "I have been congratulating myself."

Who is this man in Christ? Paul said, "I am a happy man — a man in Christ."

THE LANGUAGE OF REDEMPTION

To understand identification with Christ, Paul said there is a particular language. 1 Corinthians 1:18 says, "For the preaching of the cross...it is the power of God." The reason Paul uses the word "cross" is not because he is simply talking about the crucifixion. The reason he identifies with the cross is because that is where God identified with him.

Your identification began with the incarnation when God became a man and Jesus came to earth. That was the beginning of God identifying with man.

The second step of God's identifying with man was when Jesus told John to baptize Him. When Jesus got in the line with sinners, He said, "Baptize me with those who are confessing their sin." John the Baptist did not understand what was happening so he said, "I am not baptizing You." However, the union where humanity and deity came together can never be broken, not just for one human generation, but through all eternity. Jesus is still a man right now at the right hand of God.

When Jesus went to the cross, He was made to be sin for us. He took our condition, and the surgical procedure was performed. God put you in Christ. He cut Himself open, and He put you in Christ. It took three days and three nights until the final outcome, but the redemption story is still being told around the world.

Paul speaks of "The preaching of the cross..." (1 Corinthians 1:17,18). The Greek word for "preaching" is the word logos. Logos means "the written word." The King James translation says that the preaching of the cross is the wisdom and the power of God, but other translations just say, "...the language of the cross."

Your redemption and your identification have a certain language. You must learn this language of identification. Learn the language of redemption that Christ hath redeemed us. Get your tenses and verbs right because when Christ was crucified you were crucified with Him. You died with Him. You are seated with Him. Start speaking that language. It is the key to God's economy.

These words are a technical phrase in Paul's system of truth or doctrine that actually gives you entrance into the way he thinks. How does he think about redemption? How does he think about righteousness? Everything centers on "in Christ."

A BRAND-NEW MAN

Knowing this, that our old man is crucified with him, that the body of sin might be destroyed, that henceforth we should not serve sin. For he that is dead is free from sin. - *Romans 6:6,7*

...our former evil identities have been executed, so to speak. Our old rebel selves were exterminated and that leaves us no further role to perform as offenders. - *Richert*

Paul said, "I know this for a fact. I was crucified with Christ. Christ took me to the cross with Him." Some theologians believe that Paul had lost his mind. That should be one of your main objectives. If Paul lost his mind, you ought to lose yours! Would you like to go ahead and lose your mind for a little while?

The theologians say, "Now Paul, we know that you were not even in Jerusalem when Jesus was crucified. So either you are a liar, or you must know something we don't. You were not there because Jesus was crucified in the middle with a thief on one side and a thief on the other side, and all three of them died. It is impossible to survive a crucifixion."

But Paul said, "Christ lives in me now. I did not survive the cross, and there is nothing left of me. It's all gone. I am a brand-new man. I was crucified with Christ." Paul was showing the theologians the law of substitution; the two Adams. The first Adam got us into this mess, so God made another Adam. Jesus is the last Adam. To get rid of the old Adam, there had to be a death. To produce a new Adam, there had to be a resurrection.

The death and resurrection of Christ is a group picture. You have to find yourself in it, or the picture does not look so great. Once you find yourself, you can say, "There I am! I was crucified and resurrected with Christ! Now I am in Christ!" This is not sense knowledge; the Holy Spirit reveals it to you.

THE POWER OF GOD

There is tremendous power in the simple proclamation of the Gospel. The proclamation of the Gospel is that Jesus died, He was buried, and on the third day He arose from the dead. He is alive!

Because He lives, you live. You are seated with Him and blessed with Him. How could you be defeated? How could you be depressed? Christ is in you! Live in the consciousness of Christ in you. That is why Paul was shouting and laughing.

15

WHO ARE
YOU WEARING

One day I was watching the Academy Awards and thought it was interesting to watch the celebrities arrive in their limousines and walk on the red carpet. As the celebrities were interviewed, they would be asked, "Who are you wearing?" You would not ask someone that question where I am from. You might hear, "Walmart" or "Target," but not "Versace" or "Armani." The point of their question was to find out who designed their clothes because whoever it was, made this celebrity look really good! The clothing was very expensive and was a compliment to the designer.

This reminds me of Romans 13:14 that says, "put on the Lord Jesus Christ." You need to wear Jesus — you look a lot better wearing Him! His clothes were very expensive and He designed them to look good on you, but He needs your cooperation. You are clothed in His righteousness, clothed in His royalty, and clothed in His ability! Put on the new man: put on Christ.

PUT ON, PUT OFF

And be renewed in the spirit of your mind; And that ye put on the new man, which after God is created in righteousness and true holiness.
- Ephesians 4:23,24

Paul was not talking about natural clothes, but he was talking about putting on something supernaturally. Put on the new man who is created in righteousness and true holiness. The new man is in you, isn't he? You have to put off and put on. In other words, you have to change clothes!

Do you know what that means? It means to change your lifestyle, change the way you think, change your direction, change who you are hanging out with, change what you are watching on television, and change the kind of books you are reading.

Paul said, "You are going to have to change. It is time to change clothes. Your other clothes are stinky and dirty. You need to put some new clothes on the new man." How are you going to do it? You are going to do it by something happening in your mind — in your thinking.

MAKE NO PROVISION FOR THE FLESH

But put ye on the Lord Jesus Christ, and make no provision for the flesh, to fulfill the lusts thereof, - Romans13:14

Paul was talking about how to deal with your flesh. You cannot keep living the way you want and say, "You know, I am redeemed now. I am saved, so now I can just go ahead."

When you expose yourself to situations that can cause you to fall, you need to watch your flesh. Your flesh will go for that. It does not mean you are not saved. It does not mean you are not a new creation, but you need to watch your flesh because your flesh is not redeemed yet. You are going to get a new body when you get to Heaven, but right now you still have to deal with your flesh.

DON'T GIVE THE DEVIL A CHANCE

"But I keep under my body, and bring it into subjection....," 1 Corinthians 9:27. Do not put yourself in situations where your flesh will be able to take advantage of you and throw you. Your flesh wants to throw you through lust. Your flesh still has certain desires that you have to deal with. Paul said in Colossians 3:5 that you have to crucify the flesh and mortify the deeds of the body. In other words, put on the Lord Jesus Christ and do not give the flesh a chance.

Often the devil will say to someone who has been delivered from alcohol, "You are free now from alcohol, but you can still hang around with your friends who drink." It is almost like an addiction in your flesh. Your spirit is not addicted because you are a new creature, but your flesh still has a certain attraction for alcohol.

The devil will say to you, "If you are saved, you are a new creature. You can still hang around certain kinds of sin. If there has been a problem and a weakness, just don't make any provision for that." You need to answer him, "No, I understand what my limits are, and it is best for me to stay far away from that temptation."

Some Christians are carnal. They will go to Heaven when they die, but they still allow certain sins or habits to stay in their lives. As long as they do that, you need to stay away from them.

Paul said, "But put ye on the Lord Jesus Christ, and make not provision for the flesh..." (Romans 13:14). Put on what is in you, and do not give the devil a chance. You say, "I am in the world. I cannot help but come across certain things." That is true, but you should not be looking for temptation; you should be doing your best to stay away from it.

Put on what is in you. How do you do that? Through acknowledging who you are in Christ. Then put to death the deeds of the body. Put off, put on; put off, put on. It is a daily thing like changing clothes.

CHANGE "CLOTHES" DAILY

Changing clothes is not something you do once in your lifetime. You do not say, "I changed clothes twenty years ago." No, this is a daily thing. You did not get up this morning and say, "If God wanted me to wear clothes, He would have put them on me. I am going naked today because it must be the will of God. I was born naked and I am leaving the world naked, so I am going to live naked." That is ridiculous, isn't it?

You cannot say, "It is up to God. If I were to wear clothes today, it would be up to God. If it is the will of God, I would have them on." No, you had to get up, pick them out, and put them on. Often people say, "If it were the will of God for me to be healed, I would be healed because God wanted it." No, did your clothes jump on you?

In other words, healing is a part of your redemption, but you need to put it on. You say, "If it is the will of God for me to be prosperous, He would make me prosperous. Some people are poor, and some people are prosperous. If it is the will of God for me to have money, then I would have it." No, God did not put your clothes on you; you put them on. Likewise, you have to "put on" prosperity. That is what belongs to you in Christ. You have to dress yourself up by acknowledging who you are in Christ.

You cannot say, "Well, that is one of my problems, one of my weaknesses. I'm Irish, or I'm a middle child, or I have a bad temper, or I have this weakness. That is just the way I am." No, you have to put that off, and you have to put on the new man in Christ.

There is a process involved in dressing properly. If you are getting ready to go out, there is a process you normally go through. Most people have the same process. You get up, shower, wash your hair, brush your teeth, and so forth.

Sometimes Christians get very spiritual and say, "If God wanted me to have it, I would have it." You do not do anything else in life that way! You do not let your hair remain messed up and tangled and say, "Okay Lord, let's let it fall the way You see fit." No, you comb your hair. When you get dressed, there is a process you go through. It takes a little time, but it is worth it.

GET DRESSED UP IN CHRIST

This chapter is about changing clothes, or what the Bible calls "putting on the new man." Do you want your faith to become effective? The Apostle Paul said the communication of your faith may become effectual or effective by the "...acknowledging of every good thing" (Philemon 6). It is a continual process to acknowledge every good thing that is in you in

Christ Jesus. Your faith will become effective as you continue to acknowledge, think, meditate, declare, and act like the Bible is true. Acting on the Word is the simplest definition of faith. This process is called "putting on the new man" in Colossians 3:9,10 and Ephesians 4:23,24.

Colossians 3:10 says, "And have put on the new man, which is renewed in knowledge after the image of him that created him." This new man is renewed by acknowledging who you are in Christ. Paul said for you to put on the new man who is renewed in knowledge through meditating upon the Word and declaring the Word every day.

Daily acknowledge this out loud: "I am who God says I am. I have what God says I have. I can do what God says I can do." You are renewed in knowledge after the image of Him who created you. That must mean this new man has been created in the image of God.

Another translation says, "...like God." Start talking like God, looking like God, and walking like God. You have the God-kind of life. You ought to — He is your Daddy. You have his genetic makeup since you have been recreated.

Ephesians 4:23,24 says the same thing. Paul says you need to acknowledge or put on the things that are true about you in Christ. This is a "Holy Spirit makeover." Let's look at Ephesians 4:22: "That ye put off concerning the former conversation the old man...." You are already a new creature, but some things are still hanging on that you need to put off. Take off that "...which is corrupt according to the deceitful lusts" (Ephesians 4:22).

"And be renewed in the spirit of your mind," verse 23. Get your mind renewed with the Word of God. Then look at Ephesians 4:24: "And that ye put on the new man, which after God is created in righteousness and true holiness."

We are talking about putting on some new clothes. God likes to dress people up, and He is going to tell you how to get dressed up. Put on some new clothes with your identification with Christ and who you are in Christ.

A "GLORY" CANOPY

Then (the guiding angel) showed me Joshua the high priest standing before the Angel of the Lord, and Satan standing at Joshua's right

hand to be his adversary and to accuse him.
- Zechariah 3:1, Amplified

This sounds like the devil, doesn't it? Joshua is a man of God who is standing in the presence of God, and the devil is also standing there. What is the devil doing there? The Amplified Bible says, "to be his adversary." 1 Peter 5:8,9 says, "...your adversary the devil, as a roaring lion, walketh about, seeking whom he may devour: Whom resist stedfast in the faith...."

Do not expect to breeze through this life without an adversary. There is a devil, he is after you, and he knows your name and address. He has a file on you. The more anointing and glory you get, the more you move up on the devil's hit list! Your picture is up in the post office of hell saying, "Most Wanted — get him, stop him somehow."

When you stand in the glory, however, you have a "glory" canopy over you. When the devil tries to get in, he can't. You live in the secret place of the Most High, but you also live in this world where Satan is god (2 Corinthians 4:4). He is our adversary. He is the accuser of the brethren. The way you overcome him is by the word of your testimony (Revelation 12:10,11).

The devil is standing there to accuse you. He likes to say that you never did enough. You are not enough. What you did was wrong. What you did not do, you should have done. The devil has a whole list of things; not just recent things but also things in your history. He will take you back as many years as necessary to get you under guilt and condemnation until you hang your head and say, "I guess I am not qualified for anything." If he can get you under condemnation, he can cheat you out of your inheritance!

A GLORY FASHION SHOW

It is time for some new clothes. Get dressed up in the glory! God wants to have a fashion show like Paris or Rome has never seen. He wants to dress you in righteousness, glory, honor, and humility and let you come walking out with the glory of Jesus on you.

As you are walking out in rich apparel say, "I would like to come out here to show you what God can do. I did not do it. I never could have done it, but Jesus did it. I was in the fire, and I was going down for the last time, but He plucked me out. I want you to see what the Lord has done. He brought me, my family, my children, and my grandchildren out of the horrible

pit and put my feet on the rock. Look at this. Look
what the Lord has done!"

GOD IS GIVING YOU
A CHANGE OF CLOTHES

*And the Lord said to Satan, The Lord rebuke
you, O Satan! Even the Lord Who now and
habitually chooses Jerusalem, rebuke you! Is not
this [returned captive Joshua] a brand plucked
out of the fire? - Zechariah 3:2, Amplified*

God said, "I chose him, and he has been in some
situations, but I am pulling him out of the fire." Do
you know God plucked you out of the fire? The devil
said, "I have you, and I am going to destroy you." God
said, "Hold it, devil. I have a plan. I have chosen him.
He is mine and belongs to Me." God pulled you out
of the fire. You were going down for the last time, but
God plucked you out.

Zechariah 3:3 says, "Now Joshua was clothed with
filthy garments, and stood before the angel." Joshua
had on some dirty, filthy clothes. Those clothes are a
type of disobedience, sin, or the effect of sin. This was
something he did that day or last week or something

he did not do that he should have done. The devil was stopped, but the effect of what had happened to Joshua was still on him. He was standing in the presence of God in dirty, old clothes.

Often your consciousness shows on your countenance. You see people and they still have oppression, fear, guilt, or shame on them. Once you get "in Christ," you put on the new man. Then you can wear joy, blessing, confidence, righteousness, and glory. You are getting dressed up "in Christ." God wants you to change clothes!

> *And he answered and spake unto those that stood before him, saying, Take away the filthy garments from him. And unto him he said, Behold, I have caused thine iniquity to pass from thee, and I will clothe thee with change of raiment. - Zechariah 3:4*

God said, "I am going to dress you up in some new clothes." The Amplified Bible says, "...I will clothe you with rich apparel." God is dressing you in prosperity! Here are some different kinds of clothes the Bible says to put on:

1. A robe of righteousness of who you are in Christ (2 Corinthians 5:21).

2. A garment of praise (Isaiah 61:3).

3. The power of the Holy Spirit (Luke 24:49). Pray in the Holy Spirit until what is on the inside of you gets on the outside of you.

4. Your glory clothes (Psalm 8:5). Get in the presence of God until you are wearing glory on your countenance and you and your consciousness are saying, "I am wearing the glory of God." Then walk like you have the honor of God on your life. Walk like a child of God.

5. Be clothed with humility (1 Peter 5:5).

NEW PLACES TO WALK

And I [Zechariah] said, Let them put a clean turban on his head. So they put a clean turban on his head, and clothed him with rich garments.

And the Angel of the Lord stood by. And the Angel of the Lord solemnly and earnestly protested and affirmed to Joshua, saying, Thus says the Lord of hosts: If you will walk in My ways and keep My charge, then also you shall rule My house [That is authority right there] and have charge of My courts, and I will give you access [to my presence] and a place to walk among these who stand here.

- Zechariah 3:5-7, Amplified

God is saying, "If you will walk in the light of what I am telling you right now, and if you will live in the reality of who I say you are and what I have done for you, I will give you new places to walk."

God has some places for you to walk where you have never been before. In the authority of the believer, He has given you some access to walk in these places. He has given you places to walk. Jesus said, "Behold, I give unto you power to tread on serpents and scorpions, and over all the power of the enemy: and nothing shall by any means hurt you" (Luke 10:19).

You can say, "I am walking on snakes and devils. I am in this world, but I am not of this world. The devil is under my feet. All the power of the enemy is under my feet. I am walking in new places."

God told the children of Israel in the Old Testament, "Every place upon which the sole of your foot shall tread shall be yours" (Deuteronomy 11:24, Amplified Bible). To possess the land, you have to start walking by acknowledging and declaring, "I am who God says I am. I have what God says I have. I am doing some walking right now. I am possessing the land. Healing and miracles are mine. New anointing and authority are mine. Prosperity and victory are mine. I possess new clothes. New places of understanding and revelation, new places of authority, boldness, and anointing are mine. New places in prosperity, world harvest, evangelism, and new places in prayer are mine."

There are some places you can never go geographically until you first go there in prayer in the Spirit. You will have new places of influence where you never had influence before. God wants the church to be the salt of the earth and the light of the world. That means walking in supernatural influence over your city, your family, and your life. It is harvest time.

God has given you influence in new places in the harvest — in America, Africa, Asia, China, Central

America, and Europe. God has given the church places to walk in harvest.

There are new places of having miracles, signs, and wonders. That means walking among angels in the glory of God. When you start walking in that atmosphere, you will learn the keys that unlock miracles, signs, and wonders.

PROPER ATTIRE IS REQUIRED

Proper attire is required. There are some places you cannot enter if you are not dressed properly. Have you ever seen that sign posted on a door? There are some places that will not let you enter if you do not wear a tie and a coat, no matter how much money you have. You can say, "I'm Soand-so, and I have the money," but it does not matter because you cannot get in that place without a coat and a tie. Some places even say, "No shirt, no shoes, no service."

God wants to dress you up. He cannot grant you access to certain places in the Spirit and certain places in the harvest until you get those old clothes off. Take that old thinking off. Take those old attitudes off. Put on the new clothes. Put on the new man. It is a new day. Forget what you used to be. Forget what has happened to you, and walk in the reality of the new clothes!

You say, "I am waiting for God to do something about this situation," but He said, "I have already done it 2,000 years ago, and the closet is full." You just need to go in there and put on righteousness. Put on power. Put on the anointing. Put on prosperity!

Often we ask, "God, why don't You let me in to some of those things? Why don't You let me in?" God says, "I cannot let you in dressed like that."

What if someone from your past comes around and says, "I know you. Who do you think you are?" It is just the devil talking through someone else's mouth. Just stand there and say, "What are you talking about? I don't understand what you are saying." Walk off in the dignity of who you are in Christ.

HUMBLE YOURSELF

Likewise you that are younger and of lesser rank be subject to the elders — the ministers and spiritual guides of the church, giving them due respect and yielding to their counsel. Clothe (apron) yourselves, all of you, with humility....
- 1 Peter 5:5, Amplified

Often people say, "No one is over me. I am equal to everyone." No, there is someone over you, and you have to honor those who are over you in the Lord. You need to humble yourself in three ways: to those over you, to those around you, and to those under you.

First, humble yourself to those who are over you in the Lord. Your pastor is over you as a spiritual father. I have people over me, and I honor them by serving and blessing them. The Bible talks about double honor for the man or woman of God who has given you spiritual things. You must give such persons honor.

If they have played a significant role in your spiritual development, you must say, "I honor that person." That person may not be perfect, but give him or her honor by serving them and by giving to them financially. If you do not honor people who have had an impact upon you spiritually, the blessing of God on your life will be stopped.

The Lord once told me, "This is one of the keys to your prosperity. It is a greater key than giving to the poor or needy. The poor you have with you always." He said, "You have to honor those who are over you in the Lord. Take care of your business first with those who have imparted spiritual things unto you. When you do that, I will bring their honor on you." Some things will be imparted to you, but they will not stay unless that honor is there.

Second, humble yourself to those around you. There are some people on the same level as you. If you do not humble yourself to those around you, you will never have a proper, lasting relationship with them because you are too proud to humble yourself to those who are around you.

Third, humble yourself to those under you. Be nice to those on your way up, or you may meet them on your way down. You may say, "Oh, that person is not significant," but humble yourself and love them just like you would love anyone else.

SUPERNATURAL PROMOTION

Clothe (apron) yourselves, all of you, with humility —as the garb of a servant, so that its covering cannot possibly be stripped from you, with freedom from pride and arrogance — toward one another. For God sets Himself against the proud — the insolent, the overbearing, the disdainful, the presumptuous, the boastful, and opposes, frustrates and defeats them — but gives grace (favor, blessing) to the

humble. Therefore humble yourselves (demote,
lower yourselves in your own estimation) under
the mighty hand of God, that in due time He
may exalt you. - 1 Peter 5:5,6, Amplified

There is a "due time" when God takes you up. When He takes you up, no one can bring you down. If someone else promotes you, you can lose it all. If God takes you up, no one can take you down.

BLESSED TO SERVE

Peter said to put on the clothes of a servant. When you dress like a servant, you know you are a child of God. If you dress as a servant, you are saying, "I am humbling myself to be a blessing by serving."

When I preach at other churches, I go there to serve. I have been "cooking" some things in my spirit for the last 25 years. I have been "cooking" them day and night, praying in the Holy Spirit, studying and crying over them, and putting in the right ingredients. God says, "I have something I need to serve. I want you to serve it this morning." I tell the people, "Eat some of this. It will put you over."

A servant has access to every place his master has because he is serving the master. When you are serving the Master, He gives you the keys to everything because He trusts your heart. That is how you got that close to Him to start with. He watched you, and He watched you, and He watched you as you humbled yourself and said, "I am just here to serve. I am not here to promote myself."

The more you wear the clothes of humility, the more Jesus says to you, "Let Me give you more keys for other rooms. I want to show you some other things that are in My house." As a servant, you enter the Master's room. He grants you access.

There is a false humility with religious things. Someone told me about the man who won an award for being the most humble person of the year in his church. They gave him a button saying "Most Humble Person of 1998," but they had to take the button away from him when he started wearing it because he was so proud of it!

You may be humble, but when you start telling everyone how humble you are and start wearing a "humble" button, you have trouble. That is false humility. Many times people develop false humility and say, "I am nothing, and I will never amount to anything. I do not think very much of myself."

True humility is "My soul shall make her boast in the Lord: the humble shall hear thereof, and be glad" (Psalm 34:2). In other words, I am not boasting about anything I have done or I can do, but I boast in the Lord. I like to boast about who Jesus is and who I am in Him. I make my boast in the Lord.

ELIJAH AND ELISHA

...Elijah said unto Elisha, Ask what I shall do for thee, before I be taken away from thee. And Elisha said, I pray thee, let a double portion of thy spirit be upon me. And he said, Thou hast asked a hard thing: nevertheless, if thou see me when I am taken from thee, it shall be so unto thee; but if not, it shall not be so.
- 2 Kings 2:9,10

Elijah said, "You cannot have my mantle unless you see me when I go up." Elisha determined, "Nothing is going to stop me from seeing that man when he goes up." He watched Elijah's every move.

The day came when Elijah crossed the Jordan River, and Elisha went over with him. The chariot came down, the whirlwind took Elijah up, and Elisha said, "Hey, it is a new day!" When that mantle came down, he grabbed it. It represented a double anointing. He grabbed the mantle and ripped his own clothes. He said, "I am wearing some new clothes."

PUT ON YOUR NEW CLOTHES

Rip some things the devil has tried to make you wear. Say out loud: "I am not wearing that anymore. I am ripping it apart. I have some new clothes now." When someone says, "Remember when you..." you can say, "I do not wear that anymore. It does not fit me anymore." I am not talking about pride and arrogance; I am talking about walking in the light of a new day. People will try to make you wear those old clothes again. You must say, "No, I will not wear them. You cannot make me wear them." Put on the new man. Put on the Lord Jesus Christ. Put on who you are in Him and the call of God that is on your life.

Get dressed in the reality of your redemption in Christ. You have access to new places. Dress up in honor. Put on the glory of God. Put on righteousness. Put on a garment of praise right now. Walk in some new places. Get a new consciousness of your redemption and the calling of God that is upon your life. Do not let anyone take you down. Say out loud, "I am not taking these clothes off. I have some new clothes now!"

16

A LIVING SACRIFICE

Paul said for you to do something with your body. Present your body a living sacrifice. People often go to the altar because they want God to take cigarettes or some other habit away from them. God doesn't smoke, so He is not going to take those things from you. God does not chew tobacco, so He is not going to take it from you. Your body can become addicted to things that will destroy it. The Bible calls these habits "sin" because your body is the temple of the Holy Spirit.

You must do something with your body. You say, "I am waiting for God to do something about my body." No, you must do something about your own body. You must say, "Body, I am doing something about you right now."

Anyone who has ever won an Olympic gold medal will tell you he did something about his body. When his body did not want to run, he kept on running. When his body said, "No more," he kept on running. When his body said, "I want to go eat this," he said, "No, you are not eating that." I am not referring to people who run every once in a while; I am talking about gold medal winners. They had to do something about their bodies.

Paul was saying, "You do something about your body. You keep under your body, and you present your body to God as a living sacrifice, holy and acceptable." Then he said, "Now you have done something with your body, but you also have to do something with your mind."

IT HAPPENS ON THE INSIDE

Mind renewal begins with understanding your identification with Christ. That means that some problems in your mind or soul are so severe, they can only be dealt with at their roots by this part of the Gospel.

In other words, some things have happened to you and damaged your mind and soul so much, you will never be right. You will never be normal and you will never fulfill the potential God has for your life unless those problems are dealt with at their roots.

Your identification with Christ is the center of the power of the Gospel. It will rise up inside you and will hit the root of that behavior. No matter what has happened to you — abuse, shame, whatever it is — you can say, "Hit it right there." Your self-esteem will rise up and say, "I am a new creature in Christ. Christ lives in me. I forget what I used to be."

The world may look at you and say, "Hey, you will never recover. You will never be restored. You will never be healed," but God says, "I have a surgical procedure I can do right now. I will cut Myself open and put you right inside. Now stay in here for a while because there is miracle-working power in there." It cannot happen from the outside, but it can happen on the inside.

The same power God released in these redemption events is in the redemption message or in the Word. When you get hold of the Word and this redemption message, the same power that enabled God to raise

Christ from the dead will come right out of the Word and come up inside you!

Whatever the power of God did in Christ, it will do in you. It will lift you up. It will seat you at the right hand of God, and you will say, "I am sitting right here." The devil will say, "You cannot sit there," but you will say, "God told me I can sit here. Talk to God about it if you have a problem."

So within the explanation of the Gospel is Christian growth. You can finally get a grip on where you came from and where you are going. You know the road to take is identification with Christ. In the natural, the bridge is out, but Jesus said, "I built a bridge from where you are to where you need to go." The name of the bridge is your identification with Christ.

I encourage you — I challenge you — whether you understand this or not, to make a declaration and acknowledge your identification with Christ: "I was crucified with Him." Your mind may not get it right away, but just stick with it. It will not be long before your spirit will be buzzing. The Holy Spirit will say, "Say that again."

Now say this out loud: "I was crucified with Christ. I died with Him. It is no longer I who live, but Christ who lives in me. I died with Him. I was buried with Him. On the third day when He arose, I was declared righteous with Him. I triumphed with Him. I was raised with Him. When He sat down, I sat down with Him and I am seated with Him now. I am blessed with Him, and I reign with Him. I am in Him."

So many times we try to start in mind renewal by attacking a problem that cannot be reached with just a few scriptures. You have to get right to the source of Christianity where the power comes out and start to declare your identification and union with Christ. Start to acknowledge these facts by saying, "My faith is becoming more effectual as I acknowledge every good thing that is in me in Christ. That means there is more than one, more than two, more than three, more than four. It would take me all day to acknowledge every good thing that is in me in Christ." How much time will it take? You will have to keep going on and on because it just gets better and better.

P.C. Nelson's book, "Bible Doctrines," discusses the subject of sanctification. He said:

> *Sanctification is realized in the believer by recognizing his identification with Christ in His*

death and resurrection, and by faith reckoning
daily upon the fact of that union....

What does the word "reckon" mean? It means accounting that it is so by faith, saying, "I am who God says I am. I have what God says I have. I can do what God says I can do." I am joined to Him. I am in Him. What is in Him is in me. He is the Master, He is the Champion, and I am in Him. He is blessed, so I am blessed because I am in Him!

As I studied, I also read a statement from E.W. Kenyon about identification with Christ and people trying to grow up spiritually. He said that mind renewal or the process of mind renewal does not even begin until you understand your identification with Christ in His death and resurrection. People often try to renew their minds as believers by getting certain thoughts and scriptures, but they are attacking their minds just with those scriptures. Identification with Christ allows God to attack your intellect from your inner man. Christ rises up on the inside of you and says, "I am going to throw some things out of here right now." Doubt is thrown out. Fear, confusion, shame, and guilt are thrown out. He throws out all of that, including poverty and sickness.

Sanctification is the process of increasing in your

separation from what you used to be and in your dedication to God. It is a lifetime process. It is not accomplished through someone laying hands on you.

Thank God for the laying on of hands when the anointing is imparted. That anointing can set you free, but the next morning, you still have to acknowledge by faith, "I was crucified with Christ. I know this for a fact. My old man, the old person I used to be, was crucified with Christ so the body of sin might be destroyed, so I should not serve sin. I am dead to sin, and I am alive unto God. I am inert and motionless as a corpse in response to sin. I am dead to sin. Sin shall not have dominion over me."

Colossians 3:3 says, "For ye are dead, and your life is hid with Christ in God." You are dead. That is an unusual confession, isn't it? Get up every morning and say, "I am dead." In other words, the devil cannot trace you because you died. He cannot bring any summons or demand notes against you because you died. The criminal died. You are dead, and your life is hidden with Christ in God.

YOUR NUMBER ONE BATTLE

Your mind is where the number one battle is fought. Satan knows if he can capture your thought life, he has won a great victory. Therefore, the first place the devil is going to attack you is in your mind. As a matter of fact, he brings thoughts and suggestions to you. I like the way Kenneth E. Hagin said it: "Just because Satan brings thoughts to your mind doesn't mean they are sin. Thoughts may come and thoughts may persist, but thoughts that are not acted upon die unborn."

The devil will tell you just because you thought something, you ought to say it, or just because you thought something, you ought to do it. Many times, even after you are saved, the devil will say, "See there, you thought that, so you are probably not even saved because a Christian would not think that way." You must realize that as long as you are in this world, Satan has access to your mind.

I heard a story once about a man who asked a wellknown evangelist to pray for him that he would never have another bad thought. The evangelist said, "If I could do that for you, I would do it for myself!" That does not mean you are not saved; it just means you are in this world, so Satan can bring thoughts and suggestions to your mind. As a matter of fact, his number one attack against you is bringing thoughts and suggestions and putting pressure on you. He will put pressure on you in every way you can think and in some ways you can't!

WEAPONS OF OUR WARFARE

You ask, "What am I supposed to do?" In 2 Corinthians 10:4 Paul said, "For the weapons of our warfare are not carnal, but mighty through God to the pulling down of strongholds." You say, "Where are those strongholds? Are they up in the heavenlies somewhere?" Paul said they are right there in your mind!

> *Casting down imaginations, and every high thing that exalteth itself against the knowledge of God, and bringing into captivity every thought to the obedience of Christ. - 2 Corinthians 10:5*

He said to bring every thought into captivity. That means you must get control of your mind and your body. You must do that through the weapons of your warfare everyday. What are the weapons of your warfare? Get the Word and start feeding on it. The Word is full of supernatural life and power. Start speaking, "Satan, the Blood of Jesus is against you." Start talking about the name of Jesus. Start praying in the Holy Spirit. The devil cannot tell what you are saying when you pray in other tongues. Your spirit gets edified, and your inner man rises up. That is the part of you that is born again.

"But there is a spirit in man: and the inspiration of the Almighty giveth them understanding" (Job 32:8). In man there is a spirit, the part of you that is the receiver for spiritual things. Your flesh picks up the sense realm. Your mind picks up the reasoning realm. Your spirit picks up the God realm. Your spirit functions in a totally different realm.

Your spirit is hungry for God. Your flesh may be hungry for chicken fried steak or apple pie, but your spirit is hungry for God. Your flesh is hungry for natural things, pleasure, and whatever feels good. Your mind is hungry for entertainment and knowledge. Your mind likes to know all kinds of things, but your spirit is hungry for God!

WINNING THE WAR

*That ye put off concerning the former conversation
the old man, which is corrupt according to the
deceitful lusts; And be renewed in the spirit of
your mind; And that ye put on the new man,
which after God is created in righteousness and
true holiness. - Ephesians 4:22-24*

Here Paul said, "Put off." He was talking to born
again, Spirit-filled Christians. He said to put off the
former lifestyle, your old conversation, and your old
way of living. e said, "Put off the old man which is
corrupt according to the deceitful lusts." Then he said
in verse 23 to be renewed in the spirit of your mind.
One translation says, "Your mind must undergo a
spiritual revolution."

Sometimes a war is going on in your mind. Paul
said that you must be renewed in the spirit of your
mind. How are you going to win this war? You are
going to have to have your weapons ready. What are
your weapons? They are the blood, the Word, and the
name of Jesus.

You also have another help, which is the anointing
of the Holy Spirit. There are times when the anointing

will come on you. The Bible says the anointing destroys every yoke of bondage.

The devil will put pressure on your soul and your mind. It is as if he puts a band around you, and then tightens it. People get under stress and chronic depression. People live in this oppression like a dark cloud. It is like a band that gets tightened up on their head or soul. It is supernatural, and you cannot deal with it naturally.

You might think, "All I need is a vacation." No, you need the anointing of the Holy Spirit to destroy the yoke.

You need the Word of God. You need the power of the Holy Spirit working in you. You need the blood of Jesus. It breaks that yoke off your soul and your mind. Hallelujah! It is supernatural.

In other words, the weapons of our warfare are not carnal. They are not natural. You have never seen the devil, and you cannot beat him up. That is why Paul said we do not wrestle with flesh and blood.

When you get in Christ, you are introduced to a whole new realm — the realm of God. That is why people say, "I never had all this trouble until I got saved." The Bible says in Mark 4:15 that once you receive the Word of God, Satan comes immediately to steal it. So you say, "I was doing pretty good until I got saved. I was a little miserable, but all of a sudden — boom!" What happened? Satan came immediately to steal the Word.

GET YOUR WEAPONS OUT!

You have to get the blood of Jesus, the name of Jesus, and the Word out and use them. You have to get the Word in your mouth, get it engrafted inside you, and put on the armor of God. Put on your helmet of salvation, the breastplate of righteousness, the belt of truth, your Gospel shoes, and the shield of faith to stop every fiery dart. Then get the sword out and say, "All right, devil, I am ready for you now!"

> *Wherefore take unto you the whole armour of God, that ye may be able to withstand in the evil day, and having done all, to stand. Stand therefore, having your loins girt about with truth, and having on the breastplate of righteousness; And your feet shod with the preparation of the gospel of peace; Above all, taking the shield of faith, wherewith ye shall be able to quench*

all the fiery darts of the wicked. And take the
helmet of salvation, and the sword of the Spirit,
which is the word of God. - Ephesians 6:13-17

The moment you are born again, I am convinced, the devil puts a target on you. If you have a call of God he has a big bull's-eye right on you. Satan is going to try every way he can to destroy you.

Jesus told Peter, "Satan has desired to have you..." (Luke 22:31). This is not supposed to scare you, but to make you aware. You are not supposed to be afraid of the devil, but you are not supposed to be ignorant either. The Bible says, "Watch and pray, that ye enter not into temptation..." (Matthew 26:41). Jesus is telling you the same words he told Peter, "Satan has desired to have you...but I have prayed for you," Luke 22:31-32.

You have Jesus praying for you! You have the power of the blood. You have the cross. You have the resurrection. You have the anointing of the Holy Spirit. The Greater One lives on the inside of you, but you must do something with your body and your mind. God is not going to do it for you.

MASTER YOUR BODY

You are a spirit, you have a soul, and you are living in a body. Actually, Paul called his body, "it." When we say "I," many times we are thinking about our body, but Paul called his body "it." In 1 Corinthians 9:27 Paul said, "I keep under my body, and bring it into subjection...." Who is "I"? It must not have been his body because he said, "I keep under my body."

Actually, the literal Greek meaning is, "I make my body suffer." The Bible says your spirit pulls against your flesh, and your flesh pulls against your spirit. There are things your body wants to do that your spirit on the inside knows are not right. Your body will pull you to do that. The Bible calls that "the lust of the flesh" in Galatians 5:16.

The book of Galatians talks about the works of the flesh and lists all the things of the flesh. Your body will dominate you if it gets a chance. Paul said, "I keep under my body and I bring 'it' into subjection." In other words, he said, "I master my body. I control it." He said, "I make my body do things it does not want to do."

Sometimes your body does not want to go to church on Wednesday night. You will be sitting at home and your body will say, "I don't want to go to church tonight. Let's stay at home . I don't feel good. I am tired." You must say, "No! Body, you are going to church. Get up now!" You need to get your body moving.

When you take your body to church to pray, your body may say, "I do not want to pray. I don't feel like praying. I need to rest right now." You must say, "No, you are going to pray." When it is time to read the Bible, the same thing happens. There is a pull between the flesh and the spirit. Your spirit desires to seek after God, to walk with God, and to know God.

THE KEY TO YOUR FUTURE

When you get born again, the part of you that is born again is your spirit. Your spirit is recreated. It receives eternal life, but you still must do something with your mind and your body. It is possible to be saved or born again and still have your body out of whack and have wrong thinking.

Most Christians, instead of having their bodies under control, allow their bodies to have their spirits tied up and gagged in the basement somewhere. Their spirits are being held hostage by their bodies.

You may have received Jesus and been born again, but the reason you stay frustrated all the time is because your body is dominating your spirit. So you ask, "What should I do with my body?" Paul said, "I treat it rough."

In Galatians 5:24 he said that they that are in Christ have crucified the flesh with its affections. Crucifixion is painful. That means that you deny your body certain things it wants to do, wants to say, and wants to act. If you do just the opposite of what your body wants, you will be pleasing God. You ask, "How in the world am I going to do that?" The flesh and the mind are very powerful. Here is the way you are going to do it. Paul said:

> *That he would grant you, according to the riches of his glory, to be strengthened with might by the Holy Spirit in your inner man. That Christ may dwell in your heart by faith. That ye, being rooted and grounded in love, May be able to comprehend with all saints, what is the breadth, and length, and and depth, and height. And to know the love of Christ, which passeth knowledge, that you might be filled with all the fulness of God. - Ephesians 3:16-19*

What was Paul actually saying? The Holy Spirit wants to strengthen your spirit. Then your inner man will rise up and tell your body to shut up and line up with the Word. Your spirit man — your inward man — will do this! Remember, you are a spirit.

YOUR INWARD MAN

"But he that is joined unto the Lord is one spirit" (1 Corinthians 6:17). Your spirit is the part of you that is joined to Christ. You are a triune being — spirit, soul, and body — even as God is a triune being — Father, Son, and Holy Spirit.

The Greek word for "spirit" is the word "pneuma". Your spirit is the part of you that is most like God. It is the eternal part of you. Paul called your spirit your "inward man." The Apostle Peter called your spirit the "hidden" or "invisible man." He is the hidden man, the unseen person — the real you.

Paul described your body as the tent or tabernacle you are staying in, but the real you is your spirit. You are a spirit, you have a soul, and you are living in a body.

When you are born again, what part of you is born again? Your spirit. Your spirit is recreated. Your spirit receives eternal life. Your spirit is the inward man. Your spirit is the part of you that is born again. Paul said this over and over when writing about being in Christ. He said, "Walk in the Spirit, live in the Spirit, and pray in the Spirit."

A DIFFERENT REALM

What in the world did he mean about being "in the Spirit?" What does that mean? Walk in the Spirit. Live in the Spirit. Pray in the Spirit. Really, the first step to walking in the Spirit and living in the Spirit is praying in the Spirit. When you spend time praying in the Spirit, it will help you to walk and live in the Spirit.

What did Paul mean "in the Spirit?" He was talking about an entirely different dimension or realm. Feeling is the voice of your body. Reason is the voice of your mind. Conscience is the voice of your spirit.

Your body perceives the sense realm. You can hear your body's voice clearly through your feelings, can't you? Reason is the voice of the mind, but you still have a contradiction between your reasoning and the Holy Spirit working in your spirit. You ask, "What am I supposed to do about all of this?" You must put on the new man. The Spirit of God will show you how to do it. You are a new creature in Christ. You are in Christ — a new creation — but you must put on the new man.

AN INNER KNOWING

Paul said that if you want the will of God for your life, you must do something with your body and your mind. You say, "Well, I have been saved. That means I am automatically going to do the will of God." No, being saved means one day when you die you are going to go to Heaven, but God has a plan and a purpose for you now.

Your spirit knows the things that God has prepared for you right now. The Holy Spirit reveals those things to your spirit, so your spirit knows things about you that your head and your body cannot even comprehend yet. Your spirit knows things (1 Corinthians 2:9-11). Even a person who is not saved has certain things in his spirit. He will say, "I have something on the inside of me that tells me something is wrong." What is that? That is the voice of his inward man, his conscience, his spirit.

SOUL, BE STILL!

You will know much more after you get born again if you will learn to listen to the voice of your recreated spirit.

That is where God dwells. That is where He lives on the inside of you. Learn to listen to the voice of your recreated spirit. If you will learn to listen and be still, the Spirit will reveal things to you. You ask, "How do you do that?" You have to get your body and your mind quiet. You may finally get your body to stop, but often your mind is still going. The psalmist David said, "Soul, I am talking to you. Soul, be still! Be still!" (Psalm 46:10).

Old-timers used to call this "praying through" in the Holy Spirit. What happens when you pray through? Before you make any major decision, pray through. You should never make any major decision based on circumstantial evidence; it should be based on what the Holy Spirit is saying to your spirit. Whether things look good or bad, once you have a word and the witness of the Holy Spirit on the inside, it will be all right.

Paul said, "I pray in the Spirit." So you have to "pray through." Pray in the Spirit until you get your mind quiet and your body quiet. Get your spirit tuned up, and the Holy Spirit will begin to make things clear to you.

Paul said, "My outward man is perishing, but my inward man is renewed day by day" (2 Corinthians 4:16). How often? The inward man is renewed and strengthened day by day. So the key to your future is in your inward man. The key is what is happening in your spirit man.

17

IN CHRIST: IN THE ANOINTED ONE

We know if we translate the word "Christ" it means "the Messiah" or "the Anointed One." Paul said, "It is no longer I that live, but the Anointed One. I am swallowed up in the anointing of Christ, and He is in me."

The reality of your redemption is simply "in Him, in Christ." The word "Christ" is not Jesus' last name. Actually, "Christ" means "the Messiah" or "the Anointed One." If you are in Him, you are in the Anointed One and His anointing flows in you.

GOD'S ADDRESS

If you want to find God's address, look inside! Christ lives right inside of you. You are in Him. The Apostle Paul, preaching on Mars Hill in Athens, Greece said, "For in him we live, and move, and have our being..." (Acts 17:28). He is not far from any one of us. Paul said, "...we are the offspring of God..." (verse 29). God is not far from us.

It does not take long for the anointing and the reality of the resurrected Christ and the power of God to rise up out of your spirit, hit your soul, go out of your hands, run the devil off, and heal the sick. It does not take long because you are in the Anointed One — you are in Christ — and the Anointed One is in you.

No other religion can say what the Christian can say, "My God lives in me." - T.L. Osborn

No other religion can say that because their god is always far off, but the Christian can say, "My God lives in me."

You need to say, "I am anointed. I have an unction from the Holy One. I know what I need to do. I know where I need to be and where I do not need to be. I know who I need to be with and who I do not need to be with. I know what I have to do next. I know I have that unction. I have that anointing. In Him all the treasures of wisdom and knowledge are open for me. That means that I know where I am going. I know what I am supposed to do. I am not confused."

You say, "Well, preacher, but what if I don't know?" You just missed the whole point. Paul said you have an anointing that dwells in you and teaches you to abide in Him. In Him, or in the anointing, you need to say who you are and what you have in Christ.

THE ANOINTING OF JESUS

And he came to Nazareth, where he had been brought up: and, as his custom was, he went into the synagogue on the sabbath day, and stood up to read. And there was delivered unto him the book of the prophet Esaias. And when he had opened the book, he found the place where it was written, The Spirit of the Lord is upon me, because he hath anointed me to preach the gospel to the poor; he hath sent me to heal the brokenhearted, to preach deliverance to the

> *captives, and recovering of sight to the blind, to*
> *set at liberty them that are bruised.*
> - *Luke 4:16-18*

Jesus went to Nazareth, where He had been brought up, and as his custom was, He went to the synagogue. Jesus had enough sense to know to go to church regularly. Often people say, "Well, I am a Christian, but I do not need to go to church. Going to church does not make you a Christian."

If Jesus went to the synagogue as God, you ought to go to church. People say, "I don't need to go to church because the Lord and I have our own thing." Jesus went into the synagogue on the Sabbath Day as He usually did and stood up to read. Jesus went there all the time. His mama and daddy taught Him to go there.

They gave Jesus the book of the prophet Isaiah. When He opened the book, "...he found the place where it was written" (Luke 4:17). Do you know how He found it? He was looking. When Jesus was twelve years old, He was looking. When Jesus was fourteen, He was looking.

While everybody else was playing Nintendo, and goofing off, Jesus was studying the prophets. The Bible says, "And Jesus increased in wisdom and stature, and in favour with God and man" (Luke 2:52). You can grow in wisdom, stature, and favor with God and man. As Jesus was growing up, the favor of God was on Him.

HE FOUND WHERE IT WAS WRITTEN

Jesus stood up and found the place where it was written. Jesus had studied the Word until He found Himself in the Word! Isaiah 61 is where He started reading, "The Spirit of the Lord God is upon me...." Jesus had laid aside His powers of deity. He became a man. He is God in the flesh, but He could not use His deity powers. It would have been illegal for Him to die on the cross and become the last Adam if He had used His deity powers. It would have disqualified Him. It would have made it an illegal operation. Jesus had to lay aside deity powers, humble Himself, and become a man. He humbled Himself as a servant and humbled Himself to go to the cross. He did not use anything that you and I do not have today.

The only thing He used was the Word and the Holy Spirit. He was tempted in ways like you are (Hebrews 4:15). He felt the same pressures you feel. He felt the same darkness come against Him. He felt the same loneliness at times. Study the different emotions Jesus had He experienced loneliness, frustration, and anger. He felt everything you feel, but He knew how to deal with it. He dealt with it with the Word and the anointing of the Holy Spirit.

Jesus found Himself in Isaiah 61 one day as He was reading through the book of Isaiah. Isaiah was prophesying something that was going to happen 1,000 years in the future. Jesus was reading and studying what Isaiah had said. While He was reading, the anointing of the Holy Spirit said, "That is You!" The Bible is alive!

Jesus said, "That is Me right there where Isaiah said, 'The Spirit of the Lord God is upon Me. He has anointed Me to preach the Gospel to the poor. He has sent Me to heal the brokenhearted and to proclaim liberty to the captives and opening of the prison to those who are bound. He has sent Me to proclaim the acceptable year of the Lord.'" He stopped right there. The Holy Spirit told Him to stop right there because the other things would happen later.

Then Jesus said, "...This day is this scripture fulfilled in your ears" (Luke 4:21). What Jesus meant was, "Today Isaiah 61 is a fact about Me. I am a part of this scripture. It is referring to Me and I am here. It is being fulfilled right now!"

STAY IN THE ANOINTING

They did not have a great revival that day in Nazareth. Luke 4:22 says, "...And they said, Is not this Joseph's son?" The people responded in the natural, and said, "This is Joseph's son. He lives right down the street from us. He is a carpenter's son. He is saying that the Spirit of God is on Him and He is anointed." Then they tried to throw Him off a nearby cliff!

Do you think everyone is going to be happy when you say, "I am a new creation in Christ. I have been made the righteousness of God. I am redeemed, blessed, and prosperous"? No, someone is going to say, "You think you are what? You live right down the street from me. You are not any different from anyone else around here."

This world, the devil, your kinfolks, and your past will try to hold you in the natural. You can never fulfill the destiny of God if you stay in the natural, in your reasoning, and in your sense knowledge. Once you step over into revelation knowledge and find yourself in the Word, you can say, "That is me. That is who

I am. I am acknowledging that I am in Him. I am acknowledging what I have right now."

People will say, "No, you just need to get a cold drink and go sit down somewhere. You are not going to amount to anything." You can reply, "Hold it just a second. I am in Him, the Anointed One, and He lives in me. I found the place where it was written, and I said, 'That is me, that is who I am, and that is what I have.'"

THE ANOINTING IS IN YOU

You need to understand that whatever is in Him is in you, and you are in Him. That anointing is in you, but the key is in your declaring, "That is what I am. That is who I am. That is what I have. I am declaring right now. I found it right there in the Word. That is me; right there I am." If somebody ask, "Who do you think you are?" you can say, "How much time do you have to listen?"

Study the Word, get some revelation, and start to say, "Amen! So be it! I am in Him. I have the anointing. The Anointed One is in me, and that anointing abides in me." You have to say it. You cannot sit around saying, "I couldn't say that. I wouldn't say that. I am not saying anything." You have to say something. You have to acknowledge who you are in Christ. When you do that, the anointing will rise up out of your spirit because it has been waiting for you to say that.

Jesus will rise up on the inside of you and say, "I have been waiting for you to say that. I paid too high a price for your freedom for you to stay bound." So you may say, "In Him I am redeemed. I am free right now. Nothing the devil can do will stop me. He cannot stop me. All his demons lined up against me cannot stop me. Nobody can stop me. No government can even stop me." Paul had that consciousness. He said, "All the Roman Caesars cannot stop me."

THE ENFORCER OF THE WORD

The anointing is a spiritual substance. The anointing is really the enforcer of the Word. As you agree with the Word, that anointing rises up in you. 1 John 2:20 says, "But ye have an unction from the Holy One, and ye know all things." He is talking about something that is in you. That anointing abides in you.

You have an unction, an anointing, from the Holy One, so you know all things. That anointing helps you to know what you need to know. With the anointing, you can test a lot of things. Is there any anointing present? If there is no anointing, something is not quite right because the anointing actually comes to confirm the Word.

> *But the anointing which ye have received of him abideth in you, and ye need not that any man teach you: but as the same anointing teacheth you of all things, and is truth, and is no lie, and even as it hath taught you, ye shall abide in him.* - *1 John 2:27*

The anointing which you have received of Him abides where? It abides in you. John used the words "in Him" at the end, but actually he was interchanging that with the anointing. He was not saying you do not need an apostle, prophet, evangelist, pastor, teacher, or anyone else. All John was saying is that you are not left exclusively to the instruction of someone else.

When someone is teaching you, you have the Word and also the anointing. That anointing is in you saying, "Something is not right there, and I am out of here." You have an anointing on the inside, so watch it closely. You can go as much by what the Holy Spirit does not say as by what He does say.

In Christ you have the anointing on the inside of you, so be careful because in the realm of the Spirit much is happening. Moses went to Pharaoh and did his supernatural sign. All of a sudden, the Egyptian magicians did the same thing (Exodus 7:12). The difference is that the real gifts of the Spirit will eat up the false manifestations. You do not need to be afraid of the counterfeit. All you need is the reality of the gifts of the Spirit. They are part of your redemption.

THE ANOINTING COMES BY FAITH

You have an unction, or an anointing, on the inside of you that will teach you. That unction, that anointing in Christ inside you, is the reality of your redemption. The reality of the power of God, that unction or anointing, will teach you all things. It is the truth and no lie.

The anointing will teach you what is real, what is the truth, and what is a not a lie. Also, the anointing will teach you to abide in Him. As you abide in Him, that anointing abides in you. If you want to find God's address, look right down on the inside of you. That is where He lives!

Jesus said, "I am going to reside inside you." Paul said, "Christ the Anointed One lives in me." That anointing is in you. Christ is in you. Whatever is in Him is in you because you are in Him and that is on the inside of you.

When you acknowledge good things that are in you in Christ, the anointing comes out of your belly or your spirit. It rises up and hits your soul, your mind, and your emotions, and it runs into your bones and your blood. It gets in your hands. That anointing is the reality of your redemption and who you are in Christ. That anointing is who you are in Christ. You are in the Anointed One. That anointing is in you, and that anointing rises up in you. You say, "How does it do that?" It comes by faith.

The Word is anointed. When you mix faith with it, you begin to acknowledge who you are and what you have. You begin to say, "I am a new creation. I am redeemed. I am healed. I am blessed. I am prosperous." When you begin to acknowledge that, you will find that the Holy Spirit will say, "Yes, Amen. Say it again."

That anointing will rise up in you to bring about the reality of those things. That anointing is the power of God Being "in Christ" is not just a theological lesson. The reality of your redemption comes through acknowledging every good thing that is in you in Him. That anointing rises up to produce and to display this reality.

THE YOKE IS DESTROYED

You must be anointed in Him, in Christ, the Anointed One. You must have that unction, that anointing, inside you. What does the anointing do? Isaiah 10:27 says that the anointing destroys the yoke. The anointing destroys the yoke and lifts the heavy burden. The anointing is the reality and the power of God in this world. Christ in you, and that anointing, destroys every yoke.

What is a yoke? The devil will try to wrap things around you, chain you up, lock you down, and get you underneath some load or burden. When you begin to acknowledge every good thing that is in you in Christ, the anointing will flow in your spirit to empower you to overcome. It begins to lift that thing off you and destroy that yoke.

The devil is the oppressor and wants to keep you bound, but that anointing destroys the yoke and everything the devil tries to put on you. Where is the anointing coming from? You can receive it from someone else, but you also can let the anointing rise up from inside you — from your spirit. You have that anointing inside.

There are special anointings for the offices of apostle, prophet, evangelist, pastor, and teacher, but every believer has an anointing from the Holy One. Even though you may not be anointed to be an apostle or a prophet, you still have an anointing. You are in Christ, the Anointed One. You cannot help but have the anointing when you are in Him because He is the Anointed One. If He is in you, that anointing is in you, too. You cannot function in any office God has called you to without the anointing.

ONE KEY TO THE ANOINTING

The anointing responds to faith! Even when it comes to the call of God, the anointing responds to faith. Your faith will function as you acknowledge every good thing that is in you in Christ, and it will pull on that anointing. In Christ that anointing will begin to rise up on the inside of you to meet the challenge. The anointing rises up to whatever challenges you are facing, whether they are mental, emotional, physical, or family.

One of the keys to the anointing working in your life and ministry is to say who you are in Christ. One of the keys to your faith working is to say, "I am who God says I am. I have what God says I have." Saying brings you into the reality of who you are in Christ. If you say it, something will happen inside you. One of the keys to the anointing is your confession. You need to say, "I have an anointing from the Holy One that abides in me, and right now I am going to say what He says about me."

When you begin to say this, you are using one of the keys to the anointing. Acknowledge out loud, "I am in Him, He is in me, and I am well able to possess the land. Whatever God has called me to do I can do. I am not quitting. I am not giving up. It does not look like it is happening right now. As a matter of fact, someone told me I am not any different from anyone else, but I am saying I am different from everyone else. I am in the Anointed One. I am in Christ, and He lives in me. I am not a normal person. I have been born of God. I have the supernatural anointing of God upon my life. I cannot be defeated. I cast out devils. I heal the sick. I have God living inside of me!"

18

ACKNOWLEDGING
EVERY GOOD THING

That the communication of thy faith may
become effectual by the acknowledging of every
good thing which is in you in Christ Jesus.
- Philemon 6

Notice that Paul said here, "...every good thing in you." Then he defined it, or qualified it, by saying, "For I know that in me (that is, in my flesh,) dwelleth no good thing..." (Romans 7:18). When you walk after the flesh and follow after the flesh, no good thing will come from it, but in Christ, you are living and walking in the Spirit. So Paul said that many good things are in you because you are in Christ. When you acknowledge every good thing that is in you in Christ Jesus, your faith will become effective. Let's look at some other translations of Philemon 6.

> *...so that your advance in the faith may become*
> *energetic by recognition of every benefit there is*
> *for us in Christ. - Fenton*

There are many benefits that are ours in Christ. Would you like to advance in faith? You do not want to be the same next year at this time or next month at this time, do you? You need to take some steps forward. You advance in your faith by the energetic recognition of every benefit that is yours in Christ.

> *I pray that everyone who meets you may catch*
> *your faith and learn from you how wonderful it*
> *is to live in Christ. - Laubach*

Here it says your faith becomes contagious as you walk in the light of your redemption in Christ. It is wonderful to live in Christ! It is miserable to try to live any other way but in Him. Your life becomes a great testimony to others as they see the wonderful benefits that belong to the believer.

Other people will catch your faith. In Him victory is yours, blessing is yours, peace is yours, joy is yours, prosperity is yours, healing is yours, wisdom is yours, and the list goes on and on. You will never really get to the end of what God has done for you in Christ Jesus.

My prayer is that your fellowship with us in our common faith may deepen the understanding of all the blessings that our union with Christ brings us. - New English Bible

...full recognition and appreciation and understanding and precise knowledge of every good [thing] that is ours in [our identification with] Christ Jesus. - Amplified Bible

And I pray that as you share your faith with others it will grip their lives too, as they see the wealth of good things in you that come from Christ Jesus. - Living Bible

Your life becomes a great testimony to others as they see the wonderful benefits that belong to the believers.

You are absolutely wealthy in Christ, and there are a wealth of good things that are yours because you are in Christ. Would you like to understand the abundance of your blessings in Christ? You must learn to recognize, appreciate, and understand your identification in Christ.

HAVE A BOLD CONFESSION

You need a bold confession of who you are in Christ. Remember that E.W. Kenyon said:

> *The reason that the majority of Christians are weak, though they are earnest, yet they are weak, is because they have never dared to make a confession of what they are in Christ.*

Philemon 6 says that you need to acknowledge every good thing that is in you in Christ. Remember what the Fenton translation said, "So that your advance in the faith may become energetic by the recognition of every benefit there is for us in Christ." How would you like to make some advances in your faith?

Faith must have a bold confession to work properly. When I was studying David and Goliath, the Lord said to me, "Never run at your giant with your mouth shut." David made some bold declarations as he ran toward Goliath. In other words, David was no longer just thinking of himself; he had identified with Almighty God. He had declared his covenant with God. David did not go out and say, "I am going to see what will happen today," or "I sure hope things turn out all right." No, David declared ahead of time that the victory was his (1 Samuel 17).

So you must acknowledge who you are in Christ for your faith to work. The psalmist David said, "I will make my boast in the Lord" (Psalm 34:2). Apparently God likes people to brag on who they are in Him. Paul boasted in the cross because of what God had done for him in Christ.

You are not boasting in yourself, but in what God has done for you and can do through you because of your union with Christ. You may fail because you have not declared what God has done in you and what He can do through you. So you, too, can declare ahead of time that victory is yours.

MAKING YOUR FAITH EFFECTIVE

Notice the Apostle Paul said, "every good thing." There are good things in you in Christ. That must mean there are several good things, but it will take you a little while to acknowledge them all.

The Apostle Paul said for your faith to become more effective, you need to continually acknowledge who you are in Christ. This is not something you have acknowledged; it is something you are acknowledging. It is a continual process. Acknowledging is essential for your faith to work properly.

"Acknowledge" or "acknowledging" means several things. To acknowledge means to recognize, to think about, to be conscious of, and to daily declare who you are in Christ and what you have in Christ. It also means to walk and live in the light of who you are in Christ.

STAND IN YOUR FAITH

Many times people self-destruct. I do not believe the devil can kill you anytime he wants. If so, you would already be dead because he does not like you, and he would like to destroy you. I do not believe the devil can kill you at random. Actually 1 Peter 5:8 says the devil goes about as a roaring lion, seeking whom he may devour. That means he cannot devour everyone. The next verse says, "Whom resist steadfast in the faith...." Another translation says, "Stand rocklike, immovablein your faith."

Stand in your faith in what God has done for you in Christ, in who you are, and in what you have in Christ. You resist the devil. He looks to find someone he can devour. The devil cannot destroy everyone. He cannot destroy you anytime he wants. Somehow he needs to get you to cooperate with him. Often people die because they give up. They just get down on themselves, give up, and quit.

Many times people do not need the devil to whip them because they whip themselves. They are selfdefeated because they think about every bad thing in their lives, every bad thing in their past, and every bad thing in their present. They get depressed because of so many bad things.

In tennis, baseball, or basketball, a good coach will always tell the player who missed a shot, "You do not have time to think about the last shot you missed. This game is too short, and if you keep thinking about the last shot you missed, you will get down on yourself.

That will affect the rest of your game and the whole team. It will cause you to lose." So the coach will say, "Shake it off fast! Forget about it."

Brethren, I count not myself to have apprehended: but this one thing I do, forgetting those things which are behind, and reaching forth unto those things which are before, I press toward the mark for the prize of the high calling of God in Christ Jesus. - Philippians 3:13,14

Press on to those things that are ahead. Do you know some things are just ahead for you? You must take your place and hold yourself in place in who you are in Christ. Paul said, "Acknowledging every good thing that is in you in Christ." There are some good things that are in you that you need to acknowledge. Confess them. Your faith becomes effective when you acknowledge those things. "Acknowledge" means you have to say it.

Get up each morning and say, "I am the righteousness of God in Christ. I have been made right with God. In Christ Jesus, I am righteous. I am a new creation in Him. It is so good to be in Christ. In Him I am strong. In Him I am blessed. In Him I have boldness and access before the presence of God. In Him I have my redemption. In Him I am forgiven. Forgiveness is mine. In Him I have been delivered. In Him I am redeemed. Whatever is in Him is in me because I am in Him."

ACKNOWLEDGING
EVERY GOOD THING IN CHRIST

Acknowledging must center around four main areas:

1. What God has done for you in Christ Jesus in the plan of redemption

2. Who you are now and what you have now in Christ

3. What God can do through you by the Word and the Holy Spirit

4. What Jesus is doing for you now at the right hand of God

Paul used these "in Christ" scriptures in Ephesians and Colossians to tell you what God has done for you in Christ.

> *Blessed be the God and Father of our Lord Jesus Christ, who hath blessed us with all spiritual blessings in heavenly places in Christ.*
> *- Ephesians 1:3*

> *...wherein he hath made us accepted in the beloved. - Ephesians 1:6*

You have been accepted in the beloved, so you do not need to live with a sense of rejection all the time, feeling like you do not quite measure up. You have been accepted in the beloved, and you are in Christ. God accepts you, and He loves you.

> *In whom we have redemption through his blood, the forgiveness of sins.... - Ephesians 1:7*

> *And you hath he quickened.... - Ephesians 2:1*

> *And hath raised us up together, and made us sit together in heavenly places in Christ Jesus.*
> *- Ephesians 2:6*

For we are his workmanship, created in Christ Jesus.... - Ephesians 2:10

Giving thanks unto the Father, which hath made us meet to be partakers of the inheritance of the saints in light: Who hath delivered us from the power of darkness, and hath translated us into the kingdom of his dear Son: In whom we have redemption through his blood, even the forgiveness of sins. - Colossians 1:12-14

For in him dwelleth all the fulness of the Godhead bodily. And ye are complete in him.... - Colossians 2:9,10

For all the promises of God in him are yea, and in him Amen, unto the glory of God by us. - 2 Corinthians 1:20

All the promises of God in Him are yes and amen to the glory of God by us! What God has done in your life will bring glory to God. Put on the Lord Jesus Christ. People will say, "Who do you think you are? You think you can act like Christ?" You say, "Exactly. He lives in me, and I am putting Him on."

It does not happen overnight. There is a daily time when Christ is formed in you. You put Him on, and it begins to affect every area of your life. What you used to be just disappears. When you look at old pictures, you can say, "That person does not even exist anymore. I am a brandnew person. Christ lives in me."

Without Him we can do nothing; but with Him we can do anything. Put off the old man with his old ways of thinking, old actions, and old attitudes.

Say this out loud: "By my confession, I am putting off the old man, and I am putting on the new man with new clothes and new righteousness. In Him, I am redeemed. In Him, I am holy. The anointing is in me. I am putting on the new man with new behavior. I am walking in Christ. I live in Christ. I make no provision for the flesh to fulfill its lust. I put on the Lord Jesus Christ. I am putting Him on right now. In Him, I am strong. In Him, I am righteous now. I am putting on some new clothes. Every day I put on my new clothes."

19

CONFESSIONS: MY IDENTITY IN CHRIST

I have a new identity. I have been identified with Christ. I do not identify with the past anymore. I do not identify with the world anymore. I identify with Christ. I do not identify with failure anymore. I am identified with Christ. I do not identify with poverty. I identify with Christ. I do not identify with guilt and shame. I identify with Christ, and I have been made righteous in Him. Christ lives in me. It is no longer I who lives. "Little I" moved out and "big Christ" moved in. Christ the Anointed One, Christ the Master, Christ the Champion lives in me. The Greater One lives in me by the Word and the Holy Spirit. The life of God is in me.

Victory is mine. I am identified with Christ, the triumphant Christ, the risen Christ. I reign with Him. I am seated with Him. I am blessed with Him. I am complete in Him, in union with Christ. I thank You for that, Father God. Thank You, Lord. You performed surgery for me on Your Son 2,000 years ago in the realm of the Spirit. Oh, the impact of what Jesus has done for me! I have revelation knowledge, a spirit of wisdom, and revelation. I can see who I am in Him. He lives in me.

Christ took me to the cross with Him. I died there with Him. Now it is not my old self, but Christ Himself who lives in me. I consider myself as having died. Now I am enjoying a new existence which is simply Jesus using my body. It is no longer I who live. It is Christ that lives in me.

I was crucified with Christ. I died with Him. I was buried with Him, but on the third day, I was made righteous, made alive with Him, raised with Him, seated with Him, triumphant with Him, blessed with Him. I give thanks to the Father who has made me worthy and has qualified me for my inheritance.

I reign with Him. I am in Him and He is in me. I am righteous now in Him. I am blessed now in Him. Victory is mine now in Him. I am not trying to get it. I do not hope to get it. It is mine now. I am in Christ, and Christ is in me. Thank You, Lord, for what You have done for me in Christ. I thank You for who I am in Him, what I have in Him, and what I can do through Him. I am in Him, in union with Him. I am in the Master. I am joined to Christ in Him.

Devil, you are a liar. You are under my feet. Old things are passed away. Everything is new. I am a new creation in Christ Jesus.

Resources

Amplified Bible. *Zondervan Publishing House, Grand Rapides, Michigan, 1972*

Barclay, William. The New Testament A New Translation. Collins, London, England, 1968.

Blackwelder, Boyce. Letters From Paul An Exegetical Translation. Warner Press, Anderson, Indiana, 1971.

Bruce, F. F. The Letters of Paul, An Expanded Paraphrase. Eerdmans Publishing Company, Grand Rapids, Michigan, 1965.

Carpenter, S.C. Selections from Romans and The Letter to the Philippians. Spirit to Spirit Publications, Tulsa, Oklahoma, 1981.

Cornish, Gerald Warre. Saint Paul From The Trenches. Spirit to Spirit Publications, Tulsa, Oklahoma, 1981.

Cressman, A. Good News for the Word. SOON! Publications, Bombay, India, 1969.

Deane, Anthony C. St. Paul and His Letters. Hodder and Stroughton, London, England, n.d.

Fenton, Ferrar. The Holy Bible in Modern English. Destiny Publisher, Massachusetts, n.d.

Gordon, A.J. D.D. In Christ. Revised. Wade Pickren Publications, 1983.

Good News Bible. The Bible in Today's Version. American Bible Society, New York, New York, 1976.

Hagin, Kenneth E. *Understanding How To Fight The Good Fight of Faith.* Faith Library Publications, Tulsa, Oklahoma, 1987.

Hagin, Kenneth E. *I Believe In Visions.* Faith Library Publications, Tulsa, Oklahoma, 1984.

Johnson, Ben Campbell. *The Heart of Paul, A Rational Paraphrase of the New Testament.* Word Books, Waco, Texas, 1978.

Jordan, Clarence. *The Cotton Patch Version of Paul's Epistles.* Association Press, New York, New York, 1968.

Kenyon, E.W. *The Two Kinds of Life.* Revised. Kenyon's Gospel Publishing House, 1971.

Kleist, James A. and Lilly, Joseph L. *The New Testament Rendered From the Original Greek With Explanatory Notes.* The Bruce Publishing Company, Milwaukee, Wisconsin, 1956.

Laubach, Frank C. *The Inspired Letters in Clearest English.* Thomas Nelson and Sons, New York, New York, 1856.

Nee, Watchman. *Sit, Walk, Stand.* Tyndale House Publishers, Inc., 1977.

Nelson, P.C. *Bible Doctrines.* Revised. Gospel Publishing House, Springfield Missouri, 1971. *New English Bible.* Oxford University Press, Oxford, England 1901.

Noli, Fan. S. *The New Testament of Our Lord and Savior Jesus Christ.* Albanian Orthodox Church In America, Boston, Massachusetts, 1961.

Perrow, Charles. *Normal Accidents.* Basio Books, 1984.

Phillips, J.B. *The New Testament in Modern English.* The Macmillan Company, New York, New York, 1958.

Richert, Freedom Dynamics. The Thinker. Big Bear Lake, California, 1977.

Taylor, Ken. The Living Bible Paraphrased. Tyndale House Publishers, Wheaton, Illinois. 1971.

The Distilled Bible / New Testament. Paul Benjamin Publishing Company, Stone Mountain, Georgia, 1980.

The Jerusalem Bible. Double Day and Company, Inc., New York, New York, 1968.

The Twentieth Century New Testament. The Fleming H, Revell Company, New York, New York, 1902.

Wade, G.W. The Documents of the New Testament. Thomas Burby and Company, London, England, 1934.
Way, Arthur S, The Letters of St. Paul to the Seven Churches and Three Friends with the Letter to the Hebrews. Sixth Editon. Macmillan Company, New York, New York, 1926.

Webster's II New College Dictionary. Houghton Mifflin Company, Boston, 1995.

Weymouth, Richard Francis. The New Testament. James Clark and Company, London, England, 1909.

Wigglesworth, Smith. Ever Increasing Faith. Gospel Publishing House, Springfield, Missouri, 1996.

Williams, Charles G. The New Testament. Moody Press, Chicago, Illinois, 1978.

Wood, C. T. The Life, Letters and Religion of St. Paul. T. & T. Clark, Edinburgh, England, n.d.

About the Authors

Mark and Trina Hankins travel nationally and internationally preaching the Word of God with the power of the Holy Spirit. Their message centers on the spirit of faith, who the believer is in Christ, and the work of the Holy Spirit. After over 40 years of pastoral and traveling ministry, Mark and Trina are now ministering full-time in campmeetings, leadership conferences, and church services around the world and across the United States. Their son, Aaron and his wife Errin Cody, are now the pastors of Christian Worship Center in Alexandria, Lousiana. Their daughter, Alicia Moran and her husband Caleb, pastor Metro Life Church in Lafayette, Louisiana. Mark and Trina also have eight grandchildren. Mark is also the author of several books. For more information on Mark Hankins Ministries, please log on to our website, www.markhankins.org.

Acknowledgements

Special Thanks to:

My wife, Trina

My son, Aaron and his wife, Errin Cody their children, Avery Jane, Macy Claire, and Jude Aaron.

My daughter, Alicia and her husband, Caleb their children, Jaiden Mark, Gavin Luke, Landon James, Dylan Paul, and Hadley Marie.

My parents, Pastor B.B. and Velma Hankins, who are now in Heaven with the Lord.

My wife's parents, Rev. William & Ginger Behrman

Mark Hankins Ministries Publications

11:23 - THE LANGUAGE OF FAITH
Never under-estimate the power of one voice! Over 100 Inspirational, mountain-moving quotes to "stir-up" the spirit of faith in you.

REVOLUTIONARY REVELATION
This book provides excellent insight on how the spirit of wisdom and revelation is mandatory for believers to access their call, inheritance, and authority in Christ.

LET THE GOOD TIMES ROLL
This book focuses on the five keys to heaven on earth: The Holy Spirit, Glory, Faith, Joy and Redemption. The Holy Spirit is a genius. If you will listen to Him, He will make you look smart.

THE SECRET POWER OF JOY
This book shows believers how to bring the heavenly atmosphere of joy into the reality of their daily lives. This triumphant joy brings victory in every circumstance.

SPIRIT-FILLED SCRIPTURE STUDY GUIDE

A comprehensive study of scriptures in over 120 different translations on topics such as: Redemption, Faith, Finances, Prayer and many more.

THE SPIRIT OF FAITH

If you only knew what was on the other side of your mountain, you would move it! Having a spirit of faith is necessary to do the will of God and fulfill your destiny.

THE BLOODLINE OF A CHAMPION - THE POWER OF THE BLOOD OF JESUS

In this book, you will clearly see what the blood has done FOR US but also what the blood has done IN US as believers.

TAKING YOUR PLACE IN CHRIST

Many Christians talk about what they are trying to be and what they are going to be. This book is about who you are NOW as a believer in Christ.

PAUL'S SYSTEM OF TRUTH

Paul's sytem of truth reveals man's redemption in Christ, the reality of what happened from the cross to the throne and how it is applied for victory in life through Jesus Christ.

FAITH OPENS THE DOOR TO THE SUPERNATURAL

In this book, you will learn how believing and speaking opens the door to the supernatural in your life. Your faith will never rise about your level of confession - so get a grip on your lip!

DIVINE APPROVAL

One of the most misunderstood subjects in the Bible is righteousness. The Gospel of Christ is a revelation of the righteousness of God. Understanding you have GOD'S DIVINE APPROVAL on your life sets you free from the sense of rejection, inadequacy or inferiority.

HOW TO RECEIVE GOD'S EXTRAVAGANT GENEROSITY

Learning how God thinks about generosity will produce tremendous results! Your generosity unlocks God's generosity. When you are a generous giver, God does things for you that money cannot do.

NEVER RUN AT YOUR GIANT WITH YOUR MOUTH SHUT

The Bible story of David and Goliath gives us a picture of how faith in God is released through faith-filled words. Winning the War of words is necessary to win the fight of faith.

THE NEW

The power of the cross brings old things to an end. God has a NEW PLAN for your life. The enemies of fear, anxiety, shame, and guilt will never rise and come back to haunt you. You've put your trust in the blood of Jesus, you're sanctifying yourself, and God is making a way where there was no way.

GOD'S HEALING WORD by Trina Hankins

Trina's testimony and a practical guide to receiving healing through meditation on the Word of God. This guide included: testimonies, practical teaching, scriptures & confessions, and a CD with scriptures and confessions (read by Mark Hankins).

Mark Hankins Ministries

P.O. Box 12863 Alexandria, LA 71315
Phone: 318.767.2001
E-mail:contact@markhankins.org
Visit us on the web: www.markhankins.org

WE'RE IN THIS BOAT TOGETHER

WE'RE IN THIS BOAT
TOGETHER

Leadership Succession Between the Generations

Camille F. Bishop, PhD

Authentic

COLORADO SPRINGS · MILTON KEYNES · HYDERABAD

Authentic Publishing
We welcome your questions and comments.

USA   1820 Jet Stream Drive, Colorado Springs, CO 80921
        www.authenticbooks.com
UK   9 Holdom Avenue, Bletchley, Milton Keynes, Bucks, MK1 1QR
        www.authenticmedia.co.uk
India   Logos Bhavan, Medchal Road, Jeedimetla Village, Secunderabad 500
        055, A.P.

We're in This Boat Together
ISBN-13: 978-1-934068-37-3
ISBN-10: 1-934068-37-3

Published in association with the literary agency of
Credo Communications, LLC, Grand Rapids, MI 49525.

A catalog record of this book is available from the Library of Congress.

Cover and interior design: projectluz.com
Editorial team: Andy Sloan, Shana Schutte, Dana Bromley

Printed in the United States of America